POSTERS OF THE

Canadian Pacific

MARC H. CHOKO

DAVID L. JONES

FIREFLY BOOKS

A FIREFLY BOOK

Published by Firefly Books Ltd. 2004

Copyright © 2004 Marc H. Choko and David L. Jones

All rights reserved. No part of this publication may be reproduced,
stored in a retrieval system, or transmitted in any form or by
any means, electronic, mechanical, photocopying, recording or
otherwise, without the prior written permission of the Publisher.

"Canadian Pacific," "Canadian Pacific Railway" and "CPR" are
trademarks owned by Canadian Pacific Railway Company and
used under license by Firefly Books Ltd.

First printing

Library and Archives Canada Cataloguing in Publication

Choko, Marc H., 1947–
          Posters of the Canadian Pacific / Marc H. Choko and
David L. Jones.
Includes bibliographical references and index.
ISBN 1-55297-917-2
          1. Canadian Pacific Railway Company – Posters
– History.
2. Posters, Canadian. I. Jones, David L., 1953– II. Title.
NC1807.C2C47 2004   741.6'74'0971   C2004-903298-4

Published in Canada by
Firefly Books Ltd.
66 Leek Crescent
Richmond Hill, Ontario L4B 1H1

Reproductions of many of the posters contained in this book
are available through the Canadian Pacific Railway Archives.
For further information on reproductions and licensing
opportunities please contact: info@cprheritage.com

Design: Counterpunch/Linda Gustafson

Printed in Canada
Printed on acid-free paper by Friesens, Altona, Manitoba

The Publisher acknowledges the financial support of the
Government of Canada through the Book Publishing Industry
Development Program for its publishing activities.

Publisher Cataloging-in-Publication Data (U.S.)

Choko, Marc H.
    Posters of the Canadian Pacific / Marc H. Choko and David L.
Jones. –1st ed.
[240] p. : col. ill. ; cm.
Includes bibliographical references and index.
Summary: Collection of posters produced for the Canadian
Pacific Railway Company from the 1880s to the 1970s.
Particular emphasis is placed on posters from the Art Deco
period of the 1920s and 1930s.
ISBN 1-55297-917-2
1. Canadian Pacific Railway Company – History – Pictorial works.
2. Travel posters – Canadian – History. I. Jones, David L.
II. Title.
385.0971 22   HE2810.C2.M43   2004

Published in the United States by
Firefly Books (U.S.) Inc.
P.O. Box 1338, Ellicott Station
Buffalo, New York 14205

TO ALEXANDRE AND MAUDE
TO EMMA

CONTENTS

Peter Ewart, 1940; 60 x 90 cm; CP silkscreen No. 611. A6648.
Facing page: Peter Ewart in his studio in Montreal in 1947. A35716.

FOREWORD

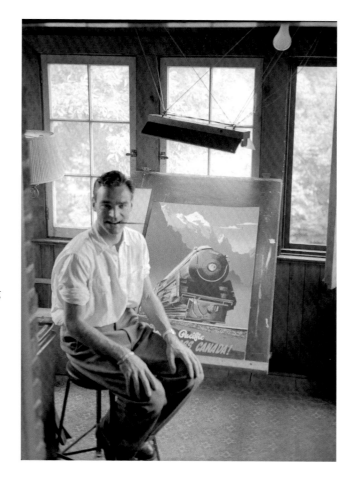

When I started out in the art world, I had the intoxicating feeling that I was going to "make it" right away. After all, I had a great portfolio, I was fresh from art school in New York City, and I was sure I had something the art world was waiting for. Ah, youth!

Alas, such was not the case. As I went from agency to agency it was, "Nice work. Leave your card and we'll call you." The phone never rang. I kept making the rounds. And at the end of a grey November day, I decided to call on the CPR at Windsor Station in Montreal.

Ernie Scroggie, the assistant director of the Exhibits Branch, looked through my portfolio. Complete silence. I waited for the now familiar "Leave your card," but instead he called in Ed Noltie, the director, and the two of them examined my work. They turned to me and Scroggie said, "We're looking for a new ski poster design, and I think your style may be what we're after." That day led to my first commission. The poster was printed, and I received my first payment for a piece of artwork: fifty dollars.

Making a living as a freelance artist is difficult when you start out, and I found it necessary to work as a staff artist from time to time. The loss of artistic freedom in this situation is hard to accept, but the experience is valuable nonetheless. You learn discipline and have to work under pressure.

However, freelance work has always been my preference. There is the opportunity to devote more time to the process, and the resulting design is usually better. In your studio things happen. You savour the moment when the design is complete. You just know the client will think it's the greatest thing he has ever seen.

Looking back over my career, I do feel a sense of satisfaction. True, I never did get to do a twenty-four-sheet billboard or a postage stamp. But I did manage to earn a fair living doing work that I enjoyed.

As for Canadian Pacific, that first fifty dollars is long gone, but the memory of the experience will always be with me. In the years that followed, I designed twenty-four posters for the Canadian Pacific Railway and Canadian Pacific Airlines.

Peter Ewart
SURREY, BRITISH COLUMBIA, APRIL 9, 1988

1885 ~ SIXTY YEARS OF PROGRESS ~ 1945

A DREAM COME TRUE

WHEN on November 7, 1885, the last spike was driven linking the rails of the Canadian Pacific Railway, developments only dreamed of that day were to follow.

Soon Canadian Pacific ships were plying the Pacific . . . then the Atlantic. There followed a chain of hotels and resorts . . . steamships . . . express and telegraph services—forming an all-Canadian system stretching more than half way round the world.

In 1939, this vast system was dedicated to the winning of the war. That has been achieved. Now the Canadian Pacific faces the future, ready to do its part in providing modern, efficient transportation by land and sea.

SPANS THE WORLD

Canadian Pacific

After Geoffrey Grier, 1945; 60 x 91 cm; lithograph. A6116.

10

PREFACE

In 1988, when we wrote *Canadian Pacific Posters 1883–1963*, many of the far-flung involvements of the "World's Greatest Travel System" were already fading from public memory. From time to time, company posters would surface, stirring nostalgia in older generations and offering glimpses of distant romance and adventure to a new appreciative audience. Few realized just how many of those posters were produced – on both sides of the Atlantic – by and for the global transportation octopus that was the Canadian Pacific Railway.

Since then, many of the historic posters have re-emerged in an outpouring of nostalgia – not only as full-size reproductions, but also on greeting cards, T-shirts and jackets, placemats, coasters and postcards – thanks to a number of organizations and a dedicated group of individuals who have embraced this art form and have been instrumental in the ongoing quest to preserve these gems from the past. For this we are especially grateful.

Among those who contributed to the publication of that earlier work were James Shields, supervisor of CP Rail Corporate Archives; Elena Millie, curator of the poster collection at the Library of Congress in Washington, D.C.; Omer Lavallée, CPR corporate archivist and historian emeritus; indefatigable private collector Dr. Wally Chung; and graphic artist Peter Ewart.

The staff of CP Rail's Photo Services Department, particularly Sidney Lee and Bob Kennell, were called upon frequently for copy work and printing; and Patrick Finn, Wendie Kerr and Ken Smith of CP Rail's Corporate Communications and Public Affairs Department were kind enough to read the manuscript and offer their criticisms.

Two of the commercial artists commissioned by CPR, Peter Ewart and Roger Couillard, were contacted, and both graciously consented to be interviewed.

For this new book – updated and expanded upon from our previous work – we are particularly indebted to Rolf Puls, director of Gallimard Quebec, who encouraged us to publish a new English version. They put us in contact with Lionel Koffler, president of Firefly Books, whose support and enthusiasm propelled the work to completion.

In the past fifteen years many more posters produced by the CPR, particularly those promoting the company's steamship and immigration activities, have come to light in private and archival collections, as well as through public auction. We are pleased to be able to include some of these rediscovered images in this full-colour edition.

Among those who helped unearth and get access to new information and who graciously allowed the posters to be shown to the public once again are Jo-Anne Colby, David Hancock and Bob Kennell of the Canadian Pacific Railway Archives; Gary Tynski of McGill University Rare Books and Special Collections; George Brandak, manuscript curator for the University of British Columbia Rare Books and Special Collections, of which the Wally Chung Collection is a valued component; Réjane Bargiel, curator, Musée de la publicité, Paris, France; John Coles from the Astrolabe Gallery in Ottawa; Burkhard Sülzen, poster dealer in Berlin, Germany; Jennifer Devine at the National Archives of Canada; and the Suntory Museum in Osaka, Japan.

We would also like to thank the Université du Québec à Montréal for financial assistance in the research phases of both editions.

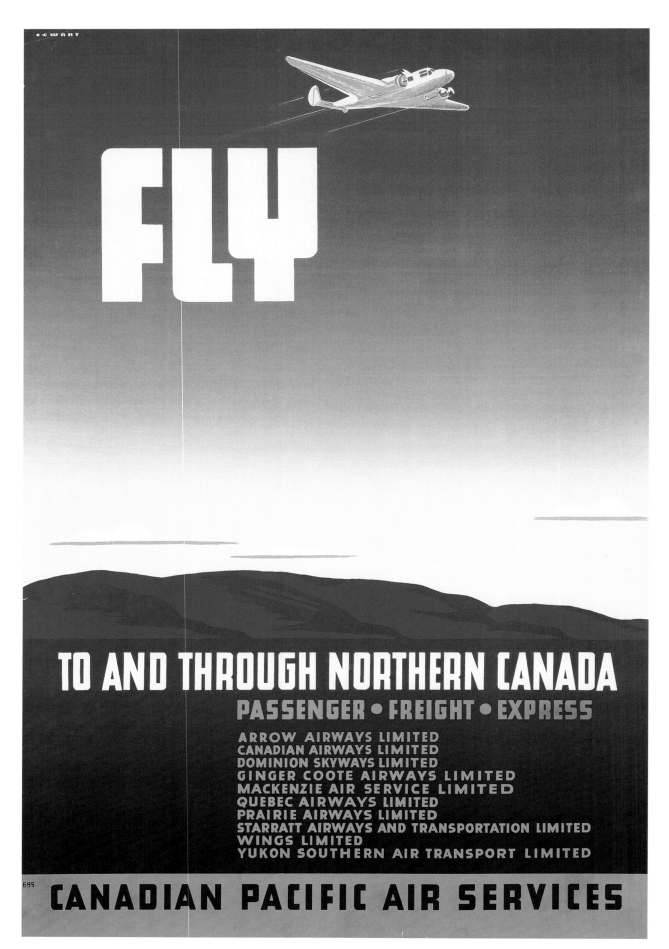

Peter Ewart, c. 1942; 61 x 93 cm; CP silkscreen. A6670.

INTRODUCTION

For the past three decades, postermania has swept through Europe and the United States. Despite the availability of all sorts of print and electronic media, the poster has achieved a level of popularity not seen since the late nineteenth century. Dozens of books have been written on the subject, discussing this art form by country, by topic, by style and by period. A few ambitiously claim to illustrate the history of the poster throughout the world.

Generally speaking, Canada's role in the development of poster art has been unjustly ignored, even within the country's own artistic community. In 1962 Paul Arthur, the managing editor of *Canadian Art* and the author of the Canadian chapter in *Who's Who in Graphic Art*, claimed that before the Second World War, "Canada was not able to support – or more accurately, had no need for – a fully developed graphic arts industry. Graphic design was hardly known before the Art Directors Club of Toronto was founded in 1948."

Because commercial art has often been denigrated by art historians, few efforts have been made to maintain records in this field. Consequently, poster art in Canada has been difficult to research and document. Many artists downplayed this part of their work, with the result that little more than a few lines about it appeared in reference books. It was only in the 1980s that researchers such as Robert Stacey, Theo Dimson, Raymond Vezina, Brian Donnelly and Marc H. Choko started to uncover a rich heritage of Canadian commercial art – one that had nearly been lost to the country's collective consciousness.

Despite this neglect, we slowly are becoming aware of the great contribution Canada has made in this field and, above all, the Herculean efforts of the Canadian Pacific Railway. The company's successful use of the poster through a period of nearly one hundred years, and its innovations in silkscreen production techniques over a forty-year period, make Canadian Pacific's contribution to the history of the poster not simply an important one, but an essential one.

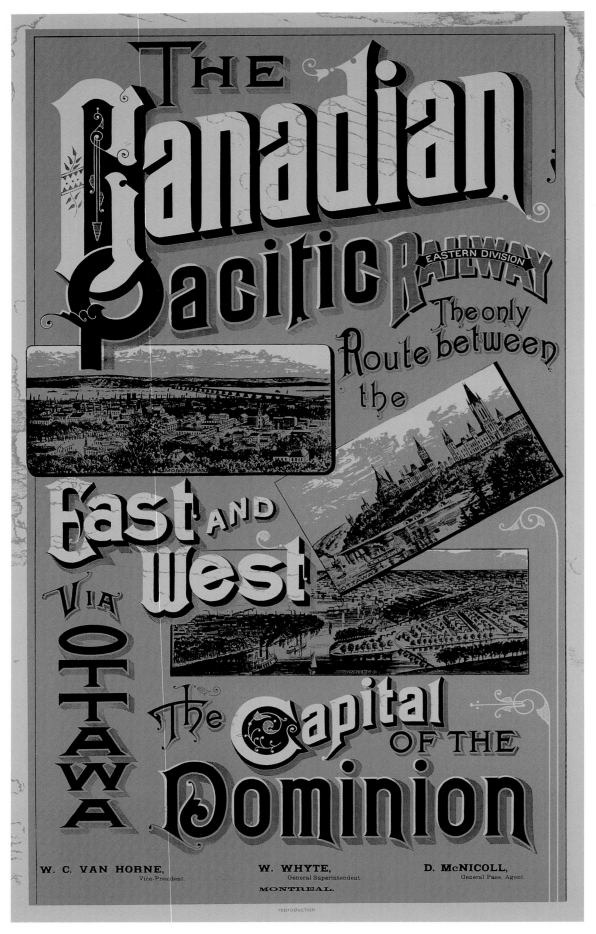

Anonymous, 1887; 35 x 55 cm; letterpress and woodcut. Coll. Omer Lavallée. A6408.

THE GOLDEN NORTHWEST

Building a company and creating a national identity

Use of the large-format colour poster in advertising spread from Europe to North America in the 1880s, and the Canadian Pacific Railway, under the guiding hand and discerning eye of its legendary builder, William Van Horne, was quick to avail itself of the new medium.

The Canadian Pacific Railway Company was incorporated on February 16, 1881, with a mandate to build and operate a rail line from eastern Canada to the Pacific Ocean. In the years before incorporation, the railway had proven more of a political project than an economic one. It was supposed to bind the country into one nation from sea to sea, as well as ease fears about American annexation efforts in the Canadian Northwest. After unsuccessfully trying to build the line on its own, however, the Canadian government realized that only in the hands of an enterprising and capable private syndicate would the transcontinental railway become a reality.

As a private venture, every effort was made to build the line in a first-class manner, to put it on a sound financial footing and to run it with the best available railway personnel. Despite formidable obstacles – physical, political and financial – the last spike was driven on November 7, 1885, nearly five years ahead of the deadline negotiated with the federal government. "All I can say," Van Horne concluded, "is that the work has been well done in every way."

While completing the main line to the Pacific, the CPR established an elaborate system of feeder lines in southern Ontario. The railway built stations, support structures and hundreds of miles of siding. Regularly scheduled transcontinental railway service began in 1886.

The first westbound CPR transcontinental passenger train from Montreal atop a wooden trestle near Glacier, BC, the day before its arrival at the Pacific Coast terminal of Port Moody.
Date: July 3, 1886; Photographer: Oliver B. Buell; Source: Canadian Pacific Archives, A.15515; Coll. O. Lavallée.

Prime Minister Sir John A. Macdonald and Lady Agnes Macdonald greet well-wishers from the platform of the official car 'Jamaica' on their way to the Pacific Coast shortly after the CPR was opened to through traffic in the summer of 1886.
Date: 1886; Source: Canadian Pacific Archives, NS.10217

Driven by the need to secure sufficient traffic to sustain and nurture the newly built line, Van Horne took direct control of the company's advertising strategy and devised the imaginative slogans that heralded the advent of transcontinental passenger operations on the CPR. In particular, the scenic wonders of the Rocky and Selkirk mountains – "twenty Switzerlands in one" – were extolled to draw attention to the new route across the continent. In a bid to familiarize both Europeans and North Americans with the possibilities of this vast Canadian alpine "playground," Van Horne made the eminently practical proposition "If we can't export the scenery, we'll import the tourists."

George Henry Ham, a Winnipeg journalist who became head of the company's publicity department in the 1890s, recalls in his memoirs, *Reminiscences of a Raconteur*, some of Van Horne's more memorable pitches:

> When the passenger service of the C.P.R. was inaugurated, the citizens of Montreal, Toronto, Ottawa and other large centres were puzzled and astonished one morning in seeing numerous billboards decorated with streamers on which were printed – *"Said the Prince to the Duke: 'How high we live on the C.P.R.' What the Duke said to the Prince: 'All sensible people travel on the C.P.R.'; 'Parisian Politeness on the C.P.R.'; 'Great Salome on the C.P.R.'; and 'By Thunder-Bay passes the C.P.R.,'"* the final four words … being in comparatively small type.
>
> They created quite a little stir at the time, being somewhat novel in advertising. Twenty-five years later, an advertising man recalled the advertisements and gave his opinion that they were no good, and also intimated that they were really quite idiotic. "And yet you remember them for a quarter of a century?" I asked. "They must have been pretty good advertising."

And they were.

Like the billboards, most of the early posters employed bold catchphrases along with information about rates and destinations. They were unembellished with any decoration other than what might be available from the printer's set of type blocks. In the first phase of poster production, which lasted from the early 1880s until about 1910, a large number of CPR posters were produced in Canada

Anonymous, c. 1884; 17 x 53 cm; letterpress. The J.M.W. Jener
Stationery and Printing Co., Chicago. A4413.

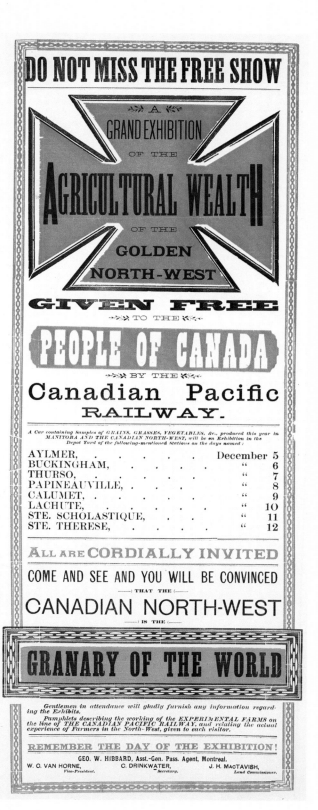

Anonymous,1884; 26 x 64 cm; letterpress. A6424.

Anonymous, 1886; 25 x 68 cm; letterpress.
McKay Bros. Printers, Toronto. Coll. Omer Lavallée. A6406.

– mainly Montreal – using letterpress techniques and simple woodcut illustrations.

The very first posters advertised rail services on the lines in the East. Revenues were urgently needed to finance the completion of the main line and to keep the entire dream afloat. Events such as the Montreal Winter Carnival, an annual celebration launched in January 1883, were prime opportunities to offer special excursion rates from as far away as Sudbury, Ontario. One of the better known "woodcut posters" announces *A Red Letter Day for Canada, June 28, '86, when the Canadian Pacific Railway opens to the Pacific Ocean.* Printed in red and black ink, it represents poster art in its infancy.

The value of high-profile advertising was not lost at Canadian Pacific's top level. At one point management received complaints about the building housing the company's traffic department on Cannon Street in London, England. It was covered with so many placards and bills that it did not look respectable. Van Horne replied, "If we can get more traffic by displaying placards, etc., in front of the present building, they must be so displayed, and if we can earn a dollar extra by painting the building yellow and spotting it with blue, it should be so painted."

By the mid-1880s, the sophisticated fine-line steel and copper engraving technology used for currency was adapted for CPR's advertising campaigns. Canadian Pacific relied on the services of the American Bank Note Company to provide the finely engraved plates on which the New York firm had built its reputation. One of the first posters using this new technology included an appeal to U.S. tourists. It emphasized the CPR's connections to Detroit, Chicago and the western states, which provided access to "The Model Road of Canada with the finest equipped passenger trains in America."

Colour posters, beautifully illustrated and elaborately lettered, were produced to announce not only the CPR's rail services, but also, beginning in 1884, the connecting steamship service on the Great Lakes. The detail and the quality of the type in *"S.S. Algoma passing Thunder Cape, Lake Superior"* exemplify what late nineteenth-century engravers and printers could accomplish.

At the time the CPR was placing its advertisements on walls across the continent, the process of lithography was being introduced in Canada, where it was put to use in poster production. Lithography is a printing technique based on the principle that grease and water do not mix. When the

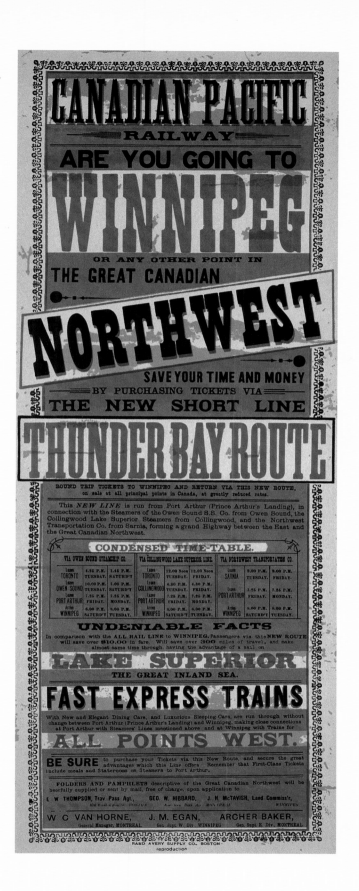

Anonymous, c. 1883; 23 x 60 cm; letterpress.
Rand Avery Supply Co., Boston. A6407.

Anonymous, 1884; 25 x 68 cm; letterpress and woodcut.
McGill University, RBSC.

The mahogany interior of the dining car 'Buckingham' was typical
of the style of accommodation for first-class passengers on CPR
transcontinental trains of the 1880s.
Date: c.1886; Photographer: Trueman & Caple; Source: Canadian
Pacific Archives, A.189

technique was first developed, greasy crayons were used
to draw or copy images onto limestone slabs. A gum arabic
solution was then applied to the stones, making the non-im-
age areas water-receptive and the image areas oil-receptive.
Water was used to dampen the stones, then greasy printing
ink was rolled over them. The ink adhered only to the image area. Finally, paper was pressed on top. Each colour, of
course, had to be prepared separately.

Soon afterward, steam engines were used to accelerate
the lithographic printing process. By the end of the nineteenth century, copper and zinc plates replaced the stones,
allowing the use of rotating drums in the press.

A rather amusing example of early lithography is the
CPR poster announcing the rates for *"Summer Tours
— 1893."* Cartoonlike figures carry advertising sandwich
boards listing fares from Toronto to points in Canada
and the United States. An "around-the-world" fare, made
possible by the company's new "Pacific Empress" steamships and its arrangements with other steamship lines,
is quoted at $610.

Anonymous, c. 1883; 28 x 70 cm; letterpress and engraving.
American Bank Note Co., New York. A6418.

Anonymous, c. 1883; 28 x 70 cm; letterpress and engraving.
American Bank Note Co., New York. A6367.

Anonymous, c. 1895; 98 x 148 cm; lithograph. W.H. Smith and Son, London. ANC/137959.

Most of the artwork produced during the nineteenth century was the work of anonymous artists. Only the printing companies for which the artists worked were credited.

During the remaining years of the 1880s, the railway was placed in first-class operating condition; the roadbed was improved, and trestles and other structures were strengthened or upgraded. Telegraph services operated along the company's lines, an express package service was introduced with the company's acquisition of the Dominion Express Company, and plans for a system of hotels were under way.

To supplement the promotional efforts of rural, small-town and city passenger agents, an international network was launched to distribute CPR literature to the emerging tourist-class market. In *The Selling of Canada: The CPR and the Beginnings of Canadian Tourism,* about the CPR and the beginnings of the tourism industry, author E.J. Hart explains the allocation of agents throughout the world:

Half the company's complement of twelve travelling passenger agents in 1889 worked with agents representing the C.P.R. in the United States. American agents too operated under numerous titles depending on their location and responsibilities, varying from the general eastern agent in New York City to the commercial agent in Chicago to the freight and passenger agent in Philadelphia. Passenger business in Great Britain and on the European Continent was handled initially by the C.P.R. Emigration Department and later in the eighties by the European Traffic Agent, Archer Baker, with offices in London, Liverpool and Glasgow. Further afield solicitation was placed in the hands of travel agencies such as Thomas Cook & Son or others using its very successful commission formula. Countries where travel agents acted for the C.P.R. by the early nineties included Australia (Oceanic S.S. Co.), Japan (Frazar & Co.), India and Burma (Thomas Cook), and Ceylon and China (Jardine, Matheson & Co.).

In the East, the railway was completed from Montreal through Maine to the Atlantic Ocean at Saint John, New

Anonymous, 1893; 30 x 90 cm; lithograph.
Alexander and Cable Co., Toronto. Coll. Omer Lavallée.
A6405.

Brunswick. The acquisition of the Soo Line gave the company a connection with the American Midwest.

In 1893, the Château Frontenac Hotel opened in Quebec City, the first CP building – hotels as well as railway stations – to feature the distinctive château style of architecture.

The period between the turn of the century and the First World War is sometimes referred to as the Golden Age of the CPR. Great numbers of locomotives and rolling stock were added to handle ever-increasing amounts of freight and passenger traffic. Some of North America's most challenging engineering feats were undertaken, including the 8 km (5-mile) Connaught Tunnel at Rogers Pass, the world-famous Spiral Tunnels and the mammoth Lethbridge Viaduct. The hotel chain underwent an ambitious period of expansion from Victoria to the Maritimes. And Canadian Pacific entered the competitive North Atlantic steamship market.

Because it distributed an enormous quantity of literature promoting Canada as a settlers' paradise and

an extraordinary tourist destination, the CPR greatly influenced how the country was perceived by the rest of the world. Van Horne was especially rankled by European preconceptions of Canada as a frozen wasteland. When British imperialist and popular author Rudyard Kipling called Canada "Our Lady of the Snows," Van Horne quickly took action. For many years few CPR advertisements and virtually no posters – with the exception of those for the Montreal Winter Carnival – were allowed to show winter scenes. Instead, the railway emphasized the scenic wonders, geographic diversity and fertility of the land. The country's abundant wilderness was promoted as a wonderland for hunting, fishing, swimming, hiking, horseback riding, mountain climbing, or just sitting back and relaxing. Not until skiing joined the mix as a feature attraction during the thirties was the Great White North allowed to show its frosty alter ego.

Anonymous, 1893; 113 x 55 cm; lithograph. A6331.

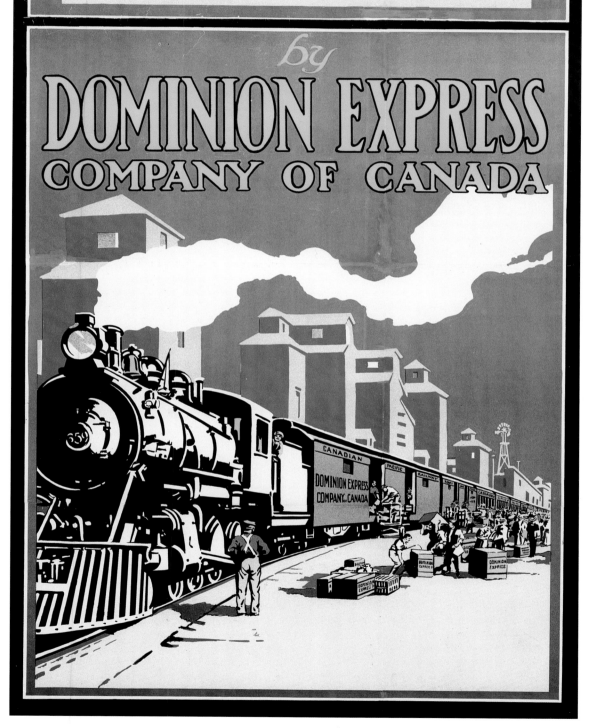

Anonymous, c. 1910; 63 x 100 cm; lithograph. A6426.

Anonymous, 1922; 62 x 86 cm; lithograph. A6008.

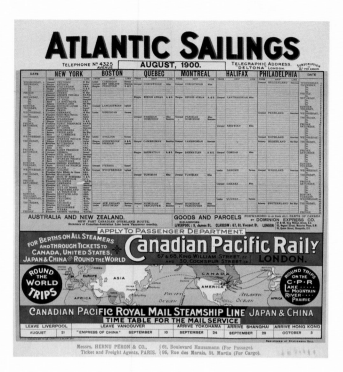

Anonymous, 1900; 49 x 57 cm; lithograph. McCaw Stevenson &
Orr Ltd., Belfast. Coll. Marc H. Choko.

Anonymous, 1915; 53 x 28 cm; letterpress
and photolithograph. A6340.

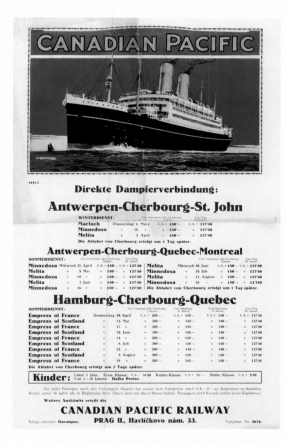

Odin Rosenvinge, 1926; 35 x 52 cm; lithograph.
UBC-Chung coll. 3936.

Anonymous, 1927; 61 x 91 cm; letterpress and photolithograph.
Printed in Canada. A6020.

Anonymous, c. 1920; 38 x 60 cm; lithograph. Printed in Canada. A6199.

BRING YOUR FAMILIES TO CANADA

Immigration and colonization

When the Canadian Pacific Railway received large grants of land as a condition of building the transcontinental line, it became the largest owner of real estate in the Canadian North-West. As a result, management focused on immigration and colonization as a way to increase the company's revenue base. The company already had experience in this area. One factor that had helped the CPR syndicate in its bid to win the railway contract was its members' investment in the St. Paul & Pacific Railway and their proven record in promoting immigration to the United States.

Even before the CPR line was completed along the north shore of Lake Superior, the company was actively pursuing immigrants in the United States and Europe, as well as in eastern Canada. Once enticed to come west, settlers were transported there by way of Detroit and Chicago, and then on to Winnipeg. To coordinate these activities, the CPR organized an immigration department, with offices abroad. Alexander Begg, CPR's general emigration agent, operated out of London. H.H. "Toe" Laer, who worked under Begg's supervision, was responsible for continental Europe.

The CPR sent Laer to thirty emigration centres in northern Europe and authorized him to set up a network of agents to handle the distribution of the company's publicity materials. Brochures, pamphlets and posters were published in English, Danish, Dutch, Finnish, French, Gaelic, German, Norwegian, Swedish and Welsh. Eventually the distribution of advertising material was handled through thousands of agencies in Great Britain and two hundred centres in northern Europe. At one point

Although Spartan, the colonist sleeping cars introduced by CPR in 1884 were a decided improvement over the ordinary day coaches for immigrant traffic to the west.
Date: 1885–1890; Photographer: J. Bruce; Source: Canadian Pacific Archives, NS.12968

the company was placing advertisements in 167 journals in Great Britain and 147 newspapers on the Continent. Paintings, photographs, posters and large-format CPR system route maps were the primary components of elaborate exhibits prominently displayed in railway stations, hotels, mechanics' institutes, reading rooms, agricultural fairs and any number of public meeting places.

Begg maintained a regular correspondence with the many transatlantic steamship companies, particularly the select few active on the St. Lawrence River route, a shorter and more sheltered route than the other transatlantic steamship routes offered from New York City. He supplied them with posters touting the unlimited possibilities of the Canadian West and arranged for them not only to distribute CPR promotional materials, but also to take advertising space in the various folders and pamphlets.

Two of the most effective campaigns to encourage emigration from Great Britain advertised "Home-seekers'" and "Land-seekers'" excursions at a reduced rate. These exploratory excursions began in 1887 and continued for several years in the early spring and late summer. They offered prospective immigrants the chance to witness first-hand the potential of the Canadian Prairies, while encouraging permanent settlement along the company's lines.

In the late 1880s and early 1890s Begg's work was expanded and refined by Archer Baker, who was appointed European traffic agent with offices in London, Liverpool and Glasgow. The promotional work was now carried out from the handsome European headquarters on Cannon Street in London, which, as Baker reported to the CPR's head office in Montreal,

> for advertising purposes ... is on the finest site in London; taking all the pros and cons into consideration, less people would see it if positions were exchanged with the Bank of England, Mansion House or Royal Exchange. Ask any four persons in the country who have come up to London, say on an excursion ticket, whether they know the C.P.R. London office, and the chances are that three of them will either know the office by that name or as the Canadian Emigration Office near London Bridge. Southern Railway Terminals, Tower Bridge, Tower of London, the Monument, Electric Railway, London Bridge, Billingsgate, St. Paul's Cathedral, all playing into our hands and tending to direct a

A party of Scottish crofters preparing to leave Britain for Canada aboard a CP steamship.
Date: c.1927; Source: Canadian Pacific Archives, NS. 8454

WE'RE SAILING WEST. WE'RE SAILING WEST. TO PRAIRIE LANDS SUNKISSED AND BLEST— THE CROFTERS TRAIL TO HAPPINESS.

stream of persons past our windows either on foot or in vehicle as it would be impossible to parallel anywhere else in the world. No government, corporation or individual interested in colonization occupies an office in a similarly commanding situation, owing partially to official ideas of respectability, to the great expense that would be involved, and partially to the fact that such positions are rarely obtainable at any price.

The exhibits in the windows of the Cannon Street office, which were changed frequently for maximum impact, were said to have been "a never ceasing attraction to the throngs of passersby, estimated at three-quarters of a million per day."

The friendly and mutually profitable relationships cultivated by Begg and his agents with more than five thousand steamship representatives were further strengthened and nurtured under Baker's regime.

During this period, many Canadian Pacific posters were produced in Great Britain. The large-format posters produced by W.H. Smith & Son of London were particularly dynamic attention-grabbers, often featuring a montage of spectacular scenes along the CPR's rail lines.

In 1910 the Exhibits Branch of the CPR's Department of Immigration and Colonization was organized, with headquarters in Strathmore, Alberta. Its purpose was to advertise Canadian natural resources and the still considerable amount of arable railway land available from the company in western Canada. Since the Canadian federal government could not openly encourage settlers from eastern Canada to relocate in the West without arousing the ire of provincial legislators, the domestic campaign was left entirely in the capable and energetic hands of the CPR. Eye-catching display cases were prominently located in company stations in Canada and traffic offices in the United States. Posters, often used as backdrops, were integral to these displays. The Exhibits Branch became the major producer and user of this colourful form of advertising, and before long its administrative office moved to Montreal, so that all exhibition work could be coordinated from one place.

The First World War and its aftermath ushered in a new immigration policy and, consequently, a new era of promotion for Canadian Pacific. In the United Kingdom special efforts were made to appeal to families. The British

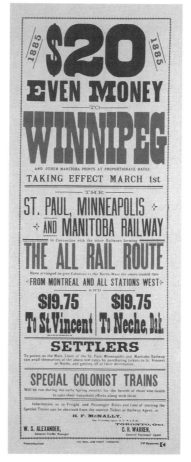

Anonymous, 1885; 26 x 70 cm; letterpress. The Mail Job Print, Toronto. A6409.

Anonymous, c. 1886; 29 x 59 cm; letterpress and engraving. UBC-Chung coll. 4050.

Anonymous, c. 1887; 26 x 65 cm;
letterpress. Imprimerie du Hérald,
Carré Victoria. A6411.

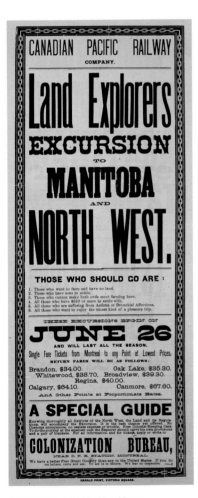

Anonymous, c. 1887; 25 x 65 cm;
letterpress. Herald Print, Victoria Square.
A6733.

government offered emigrating families interest-free loans of up to $1,500 for stock and equipment, to be paid back over twenty-five years. The Canadian government provided assistance in selecting suitable land and in settling the families, while Canadian Pacific promoted the entire program through an offer to bring British families to Canada for $15 per person. Children travelled for free.

In 1923, the first year of the program, five hundred families were successfully relocated from Great Britain to Canada. The following year one thousand families made the crossing, and the campaign continued to attract growing numbers. A separate appeal was made to British boys between the ages of fourteen and nineteen. They were offered "free passages, good wages, farm instruction and assistance to buy your own farm."

In addition to the push in Britain, similar promotional campaigns were undertaken in Belgium, Denmark, Finland, France, Germany, Holland, Norway, Sweden and Switzerland – Nordic and western European countries whose inhabitants were thought to be best able to adapt to the often harsh conditions of the West. These countries were designated "preferred" for Canadian immigration purposes, while Austria, Bulgaria, Czechoslovakia, Estonia, Hungary, Latvia, Lithuania, Poland and Yugoslavia were given "non-preferred" status. However, the limitations of this discriminatory Canadian immigration policy led to a revision for emigrants from eastern and southern Europe, as explained in *Building the Canadian West*, Professor J.B. Hedges' study of Canadian Pacific's land policy in the Northwest:

On September 1, 1925, the Dominion Government, through the Minister of Immigration and Colonization, entered into the so-called "Railways Agreement" with the Canadian Pacific and the Canadian National Railways. Designed to avoid all duplication of effort between the government and the railways in the conduct of immigration work in the non-preferred countries, the railways' agreement was a recognition by Ottawa authorities of the fact that the railway companies had a "special interest in the settlement of available unoccupied lands" and by reason of their "transportation facilities by land and sea" were specially "qualified to procure, select and settle immigrants" on the land.

After the policy was changed, the CPR produced posters in the languages of the "non-preferred" countries, and the concept of preferential status for western and northern European countries faded from Canadian immigration policy.

To assist the immigrants, the CPR's Immigration Department was separated, for several years, from the newly created Department of Colonization and Development. This new department's chief concern was not *getting* people to Canada, but *keeping* them in the country. It sought to ease the transition for settlers by educating them about the effective and proven agricultural practices developed, in part, on the CPR's own experimental farms in the Northwest. The railway needed farmers, whether they settled along the line singly or by family, clan or organized colony.

The department maintained a Montreal-based publicity branch, which prepared all the advertising literature for distribution in Canada, the United States and Europe. A bureau of information in Montreal, with branch offices in London and Chicago, had as its slogan: "Ask the Canadian Pacific about Canada."

The Exhibits Branch was equally busy, preparing and installing elaborate displays in the company's offices and at agricultural and industrial exhibitions. The branch updated advertising material monthly.

The Second World War brought much of this activity to a halt, with many of the CPR's European offices forced to close as Axis forces advanced across the continent.

Following the war, Canadian Pacific reduced its direct involvement with immigration, its work largely taken over by the federal and provincial governments. CPR's Department of Immigration and Colonization – having kicked in about two dollars for every government dollar spent during the aggressive period of Canadian immigration – ceased its activities and closed its doors.

Canadian Pacific Railway Co. agency in Basel, Switzerland, about 1925.
Source: Canadian Pacific Archives. A8051.

HOMESEEKERS FARES TO WESTERN CANADA

Round Trip Tickets on Sale Every Day

MARCH 1 to SEPT. 30

Via all rail route or via Monday's steamer from Owen Sound

Reduced Fares

Return limit 2 Months. Extension of time limit can be arranged

Stopover privileges Hurkett, Ont., Dryden, Ont., and intermediate stations, also at Winnipeg and West

For Fares and other particulars apply to any Agent of the

THROUGH TOURIST SLEEPING CARS

CANADIAN PACIFIC

Anonymous, c. 1910; 57 x 85 cm; lithograph. A6201.

Anonymous, c. 1920; 41 x 64 cm; lithograph. David Allen & Sons Ltd., 180 Fleet St., London. UBC-Chung coll. 4045.

Anonymous, c. 1920; 64 x 101 cm; lithograph; Eyre & Spottiswoode, Ltd., H.M. Printers, London.

Harry Hudson Rodmell, 1920; 56 x 80 cm; lithograph. UBC-Chung coll. 2926.

Odin Rosenvinge, after 1922; 62 x 101 cm; lithograph. A6592,
Canadian Pacific inscription was pasted over CPOS after the name change in 1922.

Odin Rosenvinge, c. 1920; 62 x 101 cm; lithograph.
A6597.

Odin Rosenvinge, c. 1920; 62 x 101 cm; lithograph.
A6578.

Odin Rosenvinge, c. 1920; 62 x 101 cm; lithograph.
A6594.

Odin Rosenvinge, c. 1920; 62 x 101 cm; lithograph.
A6595.

Anonymous, 1929; 60 x 90 cm; lithograph. Lithographed in Canada. A6343.

Anonymous, c. 1933; 35 x 48 cm; CP silkscreen No. 126. A6198.

Anonymous, c. 1925; original unknown/NS 4313.

Anonymous, c. 1925; original unknown/NS 4316.

Anonymous, c. 1925; original unknown/NS 4321.

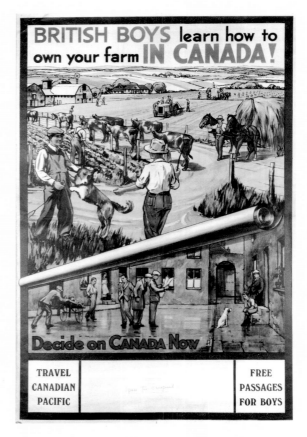

Anonymous, c. 1925; original unknown/NS 4319.

Fred Gardner, c. 1920; 58 x 95 cm; lithograph. A6200.

Clement Dane Studio, 1932; 63 x 101 cm; lithograph. Baynard Press, London. Courtesy of Burkhard Sülzen, Berlin.

THE FIVE-DAY ATLANTIC GIANTESS

Empresses and Duchesses rule the North Atlantic

In 1886 Canadian Pacific chartered its first ocean-going steamships between Vancouver and the Orient. Five years later, the company's own "Empress" steamships were providing a monthly service on the Pacific.

By 1903 the CPR was prepared to intervene directly in the North Atlantic steamship business. The company's program had made a large contribution to the spike in immigrant traffic, as attested to by a report in the shipping journal *Lloyd's List* on April 7, 1903:

> Evidence of the great "treck" [*sic*] to Canada has been very patent in the streets of Liverpool during the last few weeks. Crowds of emigrants of all nationalities have been thronging the streets and outside offices of the several steamship companies engaged in the Atlantic Trade. There have been large numbers of people waiting whilst their tickets were procured.

However, as successful as the established arrangements were, the need to constantly negotiate with the various transatlantic steamship lines to issue convenient and affordable "through-rate" tickets from Great Britain to the Canadian North-West had become an impediment to long-term financial planning for the CPR.

In 1903, with the sale of fifteen ships — eight devoted primarily to the passenger trade — the British Elder Dempster Line handed CPR the last link in its transportation chain from Britain to the Orient. Canadian Pacific would go on to be a force to reckon with on the North Atlantic, and continue to offer reasonable, packaged

An advertising display, featuring the flagship *Empress of Britain*.
Source: Canadian Pacific Archives, A6082.

The first-class "Mayfair Lounge" on the CP transatlantic steamship *Empress of Britain.*
Date: 1931; Source: Canadian Pacific Archives, A.10152

rates, in its own best interest as well as that of the new Canadians.

On February 23, 1903, CPR president Thomas Shaughnessy made a decisive move to complete the CPR's transportation chain from Britain to the Orient. The company announced that it had bought eight passenger and seven cargo liners from the British Elder Dempster Line.

With one bold stroke, the CPR entered the competitive North Atlantic steamship trade, giving it a two-fold reason to sell its services: to settle its lands in the West and profit from the European immigrant traffic to Canada. Neither endeavour was terribly profitable initially, so once again, as was the case on the Pacific, Canadian and British postal contracts were essential to the viability of the service.

In 1906, CPR launched two new fast passenger liners, *Empress of Britain* and *Empress of Ireland*, in direct competition with the prestigious Allan Line's speedy turbine steamships *Victorian* and *Virginian.* Capable of 18 knots and better, these impressive new vessels on the Atlantic scene were featured prominently in Canadian Pacific's promotional campaigns. As a result they became the frequent subject of the poster artists.

The company's resolve to be the dominant force in the St. Lawrence–Atlantic steamship trade was confirmed in 1909, when CPR purchased a majority interest in the Allan Line. For the next six years, though under one management and operational infrastructure, Canadian Pacific Railway Steamships and Allan Line Steamships were advertised separately, maintaining an illusion of competition on the North Atlantic run to Canada.

In 1915, the steamship services of Canadian Pacific were reorganized as Canadian Pacific Ocean Services (C.P.O.S.). The Allan Line service – inaugurated between Glasgow, Scotland and Quebec with the arrival in Canada of the brig *Jean*, in 1819 – was ended, in name as in fact.

In 1922, the entire fleet was again reorganized, this time as the Canadian Pacific Steamship Company. It was the dominant force on the Canadian route to Europe, with impressive reach and influence to match its status on the Pacific; but just one of many operating departments of the CPR.

A veritable royal family of elegant and fast steamships crisscrossed the North Atlantic in increasingly large numbers. During Edward Beatty's twenty-five year presidency – including nearly the entire period between the two world wars – the CPR launched twenty-three ships. It's the classic period of steamship poster design.

With flat demand for passage at the "leisure class" end of the market and decreased immigrant traffic at the other, the middle class or "tourist" market became the predominant target audience. The posters for the CPR's "Duchess" ships, in particular, started to offer services that weren't "third-class," but rather "cabin class," a designation first used in the 1910s by CPR, or "tourist class." Many of the ships spent the winter months sailing in warmer waters, on cruises to the West Indies, the Mediterranean and around the world. Again, it was the burgeoning tourist class that made it all possible – a reality reflected increasingly in the poster designs, slogans and catchphrases. Humour was reintroduced.

The Canadian Pacific ocean fleets were expanded to handle the transatlantic and transpacific services as well as the cruise business that was carried on around the world.

In the late 1920s, the "Duchess" one-class ships were

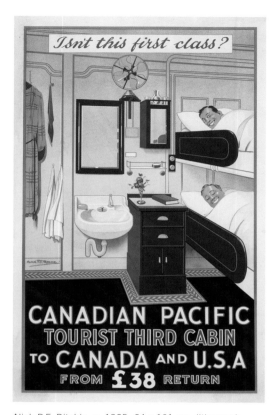

Alick P.F. Ritchie, c. 1925; 64 x 101 cm; lithograph. UBC-Chung coll. 3974.

Harry Hudson Rodmell, c. 1925; 33 x 72 cm; lithograph. Courtesy Burkhard Sülzen, Berlin.

launched to provide the extra capacity for the tourist trade, and in 1930, despite the Depression, the company's flagship *Empress of Britain* was launched. The largest ship ever to sail under the company's flag, it enhanced Canadian Pacific's image wherever it appeared on its around-the-world cruises.

In the same way the company's popular ships to the Orient were widely known as the "Empresses of the Pacific," four prominent CPR liners launched in 1927 and 1928 were collectively referred to as "Duchesses of the Atlantic." The posters carried the simple but effective message: "Newest and Largest to Montreal and Quebec." The relative safety and comfort of the St. Lawrence route was emphasized as merely "four days open sea" on "the mighty water boulevard to Europe."

CPR's Beatty was the first Canadian-born president of the CPR, and he took great pride in flying not only the national flag, but particularly the CPR house flag, in the major ports of the world.

To compete with such majestic ships as the Cunard Line's *Aquitania*, the French Line's *Ile de France*, and the United States Line's *Leviathan,* Canadian Pacific Steamships launched the 45,000-ton *Empress of Britain* in 1930, the second ship to bear the name. A somewhat bulky-looking three-funnelled vessel, claimed by some of its admirers to be the most luxuriously appointed ship to have ever sailed, it was the largest ship operated by Canadian Pacific, and proudly took its place as the flagship of the fleet.

Company posters and brochures heralded its arrival as the "Five-day Atlantic Giantess" – a reference to its quick crossing time – "Canada's Challenger" and "The World's Wondership."

Certainly the most photographed and illustrated of the company's vessels, the *Empress of Britain* was the subject of numerous posters produced on both sides of the Atlantic. Often the ship was drawn oversized in the style of the times to emphasize its grandeur, completely overshadowing the tugboats, trains or passengers that appeared in the foreground. In one example, galloping horses pull Neptune's chariot through the foam in the wake of her bow. Another, with tennis courts and swimming pool clearly visible, simply says, "more space per first-class passenger than any other ship."

The poster production required to advertise *Empress of Britain*'s many sailings and cruises through the years was prodigious. The many examples extant offer an interesting cross-section of divergent graphic styles in the Thirties.

But a far more productive period followed the war, drawing increasingly on the resources of Canadian Pacific's London office and its European network. Some of the most famous British designers from the creative era between the late 1920s and the early 1930s were commissioned by the London director of publicity for the Canadian Pacific, C.W. Stokes, to create the company's poster art.

Names of famous British artists such as Alfred C. Leighton, Leonard Richmond, Kenneth Shoesmith and Tom Purvis helped to bring this production to the attention of the well-established and influential graphic art magazines of the time, which often illustrated their articles with Canadian Pacific designs.

The increased interest in commercial art was reflected in the number of new publications that were devoted to the subject. *Gebrauchsgraphik* started to publish in 1924 in Germany. In 1927 it changed its name to *International Advertising Art,* and began to be distributed in Europe and North America. *Poster and Publicity* (later *Modern Publicity*) and *Commercial Art* (later *Commercial Art and Industry* and *Art and Industry*) were both issued in England, beginning in the mid-1920s.

In the introduction of the 1933–1934 issue of *Modern Publicity,* Canadian Pacific is acknowleged as a patron of the graphic artists:

> In fact, a very high tribute must be paid both to the artists used by the railway companies and some of the larger companies which are in a sense national institutions in England, and to the controllers of advertising who so effectively use them. We would mention among the latter, Mr. C. Dandridge, of the L.N.E.R., Mr. Grasemann, of the Southern Railway, Mr. G.W. Duncan of the London Passenger Transport Board, Mr. J. Beddington, of Shell-Mex (who had made an adventurous and very successful choice of artists), and Mr. C. Stokes of the Canadian Pacific Railway.

The Technique of the Poster, written by Leonard Richmond in 1933, not only featured a chapter by C.W. Stokes on Canadian Pacific's work in the field, but included several of the company's posters in black and white and in color.

Harry Hudson Rodmell, 1921; 58 x 95 cm; lithograph. A6021.

Anonymous, c. 1931; 63 x 98 cm; lithograph.
Hammond and Griffiths Ltd., London. ANC. 137962.

Anonymous, c. 1910; 64 x 87 cm; lithograph. UBC-Chung coll. 3924.

Bernard Gribble, c. 1923; 64 x 101 cm; lithograph. Eyre and Spottiswoode Ltd., H.M. Printers, London. UBC-Chung coll. 3930.

Leonard Richmond, c. 1930; 64 x 101 cm; lithograph. Eyre & Spottiswoode Ltd., H.M. Printers, London. UBC-Chung coll. 3942.

Norman Wilkinson, 1927; 60 x 90 cm, lithograph. Lithographed in Canada. A6016.

Odin Rosenvinge, c. 1930; 55 x 96 cm; lithograph. Turner & Dunnett Litho's, Liverpool & London. A6352.

ALLAN LINE
ROYAL MAIL

James S. Mann

TURBINE·QUADRUPLE SCREWS·18,000 TONS (TWO BUILDING)

TO AND FROM CANADA.

For full particulars apply to

SERCOMBE & HAYES,

Emigration & Shipping Agents, 9, South Street, DORCHESTER.

TURNER & DUNNETT, LITHO? LIVERPOOL & LONDON.

James S. Mann, c. 1913; 69 x 107 cm; lithograph. Turner Dunnett Litho, Liverpool & London. UBC-Chung coll. 3968.

A.W. Ashburner, c. 1925; 50 x 75 cm; lithograph. A6718.

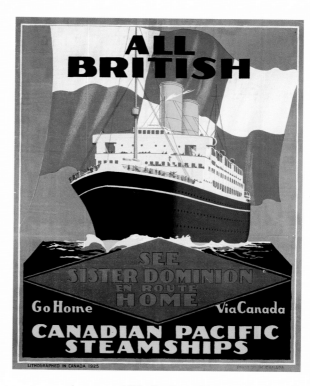

Anonymous, 1925; 41 x 51 cm; lithograph.
Lithographed in Canada 1925. A6094.

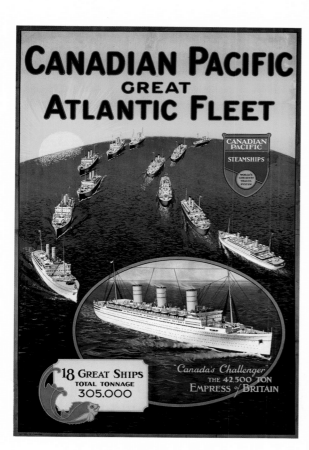

H.B., c. 1932; 60 x 90 cm; lithograph.
Lithographed in Canada. A6015.

E. Hamilton, c. 1925; 62 x 103 cm; lithograph.
UBC-Chung coll. 3938.

Harry Hudson Rodmell, c. 1920; 50 x 75 cm; lithograph. A6341.

Percy Angelo Staynes, c. 1929; 63 x 100 cm; lithograph. A6026.

Kenneth Shoesmith, 1933; 60 x 88 cm; lithograph. A6044.

Anonymous, c. 1929; 76 x 102 cm; lithograph. Lithographed in Canada. McGill University, RBSC.

Anonymous, c. 1930; 60 x 90 cm; lithograph. Lithographed in Canada. A6038.

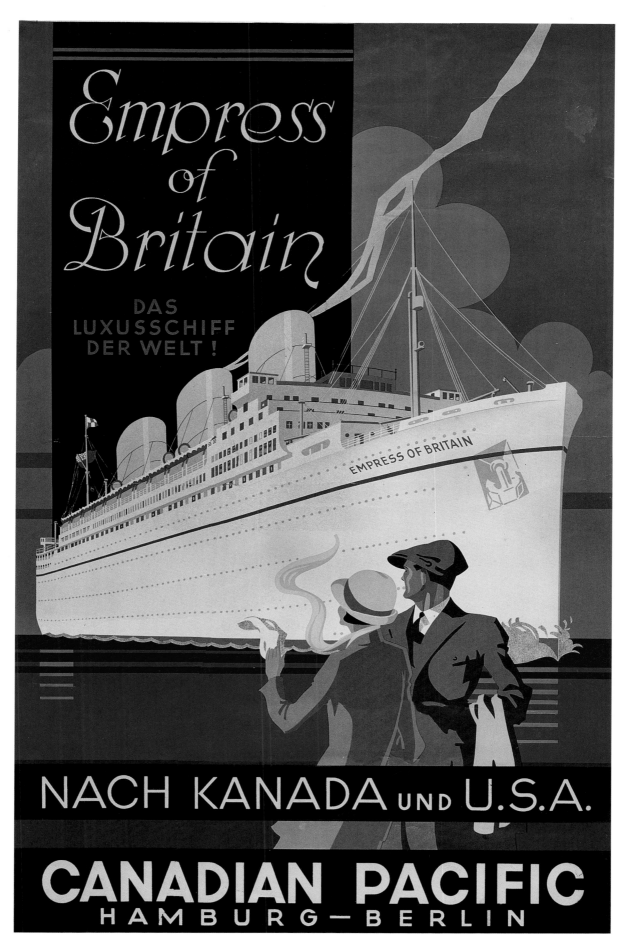

Robert Schroder, c. 1932; 58 x 88 cm; lithograph. Kunstanstalt Gehr, Sülter, Hamburg. Courtesy of Wally Chung.

Schlisinger, 1936; 61 x 92 cm; CP silkscreen. A6586.

Occasionally, misprints like this escaped the silkscreen studio. The poster was upside down for the application of the black lettering.

Norman Fraser, 1937; 37 x 50 cm; CP silkscreen No. 340. A6057.

Anonymous, c. 1936; 62 x 90 cm; lithograph. Printed in Great Britain. A6018.

THE WORLD'S GREATEST TRAVEL SYSTEM

Luxury cruises in the 1920s and 1930s

The postwar era was a period of feverish competition between the Canadian Pacific Railway and its new Crown-owned competitor, Canadian National Railways. An extraordinary amount of mileage was added to both systems through the construction of branch lines honeycombing the Prairies. Competition to offer the public the most sumptuous passenger cars and the most luxurious hotels threatened to bring both railways to the brink of financial ruin.

Between 1918 and the outbreak of the Second World War in 1939, Canadian Pacific's activities achieved worldwide status through the advent of the steamship cruise service, the expansion of services on the Pacific and the aggressive new promotion of Canadian tourism. The unprecedented growth was reflected in the company's slogans: "CPR Spans the World" (1910) and "Bridging 2 Oceans, Linking 4 Continents" and "The World's Greatest Highway" (both 1924). By 1927 CPR was promoting itself as "The World's Greatest Travel System." Appropriately, Canadian Pacific's advertising posters were dynamic classics of poster design.

Numerous posters tempted the public with the lure of the Far East. "Go Empress to the Orient," was one phrase used. "Japan-China-Philippines by Canadian Pacific" and "Largest and Fastest to the Orient" were others. The length of the trip to the Orient, with many days at sea and several ports of call, provided a sense of a scenic cruise rather than a routine ocean crossing.

The company's Pacific clientele consisted primarily of Europeans and North Americans living in Asia — commercial travellers, government officials, missionaries, students and tourists. With the exception of a government-

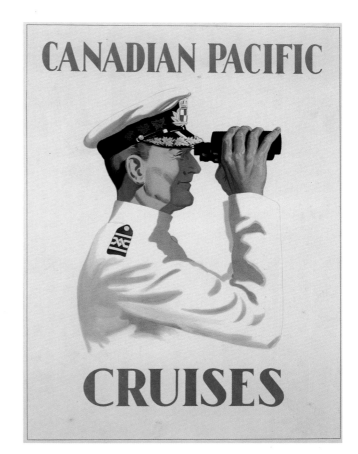

Anonymous, c. 1925; 40 x 55 cm; lithograph. A6095.

After Tom Purvis, 1937; 35 x 48 cm; CP silkscreen No. 327. A6073.

restricted number of Japanese, Asians were not permitted to immigrate to Canada. Those using Canadian Pacific services were sailing between Far Eastern ports, travelling to work projects in North America, or passing through Canada on the way to other destinations. Still, their numbers were sufficient to warrant various posters and a good amount of accompanying literature printed in both Japanese and Chinese.

The company maintained offices in Hong Kong, Kobe, Manila, Shanghai, Tokyo and Yokohama. The agencies in Hong Kong and Shanghai both occupied prime waterfront locations.

As an important link in the transportation network of the British Empire, the Canadian Pacific Railway with its steamship connections often promoted itself as "The Imperial Highway." The Pacific steamship service was looked upon as the last leg of the "All-Red Route" from the Mother Country to the Orient, a reference to the common practice on maps of colouring countries of the Empire in red.

In the period between the two world wars, Canadian Pacific ran a total of 363 cruises to the West Indies, the Mediterranean, the Canary Islands, Scandinavia and around the world. The company's first involvement in the cruise business was in 1922, when the Frank C. Clark Travel Agency of New York chartered the *Empress of Scotland* and the *Empress of France* for Mediterranean cruises. In the same year, Canadian Pacific operated two cruises of its own to the West Indies.

The next year, Frank Clark successfully ran an around-the-world cruise with the *Empress of France,* and from 1924 on Canadian Pacific ran all its cruises independently. "Happy Cruises – Popular Prices" the posters proclaimed. One important development that helped build the company's global tour business was the improved trans-Siberian rail service that followed the Russian revolution, providing another potential link in around-the-world itineraries.

Beginning in 1931, Duchess "miniature cruises" were advertised from Montreal and Quebec to New York. Canadian Pacific experimented with photolithographic techniques to illustrate its "St. Lawrence Seaway 9-day Cruises" poster. Across the Atlantic, eight- to fourteen-day cruises – often advertised as "£-a-day" cruises – were offered from U.K. ports to the North African coast, Spain and the Canary Islands. "Come with us on a Mediterranean Cruise" read one poster announcing the service. This time the message was supplemented by a

Tom Purvis, 1937; 60 x 90 cm; lithograph. Printed in Great Britain. A6067.

photograph of smiling and waving passengers, an early example of a photo-design technique that eventually would marginalize and temporarily exile graphic artists.

Another campaign touted the merits of the "St. Lawrence Route to Europe." Many Canadian Pacific ships were built in Scotland, and there they often returned with Scottish expatriates visiting relatives. The "thirty-nine percent less ocean" offered by the St. Lawrence route was presented in one poster by a sailor explaining to a young boy: "Aye lad! It's a third less ocean"; and, in another,

by a smiling couple sitting next to each other on deck, untroubled by a rough passage, all beneath the written assurance that Canadian Pacific provided the "Romance Route to Europe."

Not even the stock market crash in 1929 or the Depression, which dragged on through the Dirty Thirties, could put a stop to the expanding tourism business.

Norman Fraser, 1937; 61 x 91 cm; CP silkscreen No. 324. Printed in Canada by Exhibits Branch, CPR. A6587.

Kenneth Shoesmith, c. 1930; 60 x 90 cm; lithograph. A6040.

Anonymous, c. 1935; 62 x 100 cm; lithograph. A6028.

Norman Fraser, 1936; 60 x 90 cm; CP silkscreen No. 277. Reprinted c. 1943 under No. 754. A6371.

Norman Fraser, c. 1939; 63 x 92 cm;
CP silkscreen No. 488. A6372.

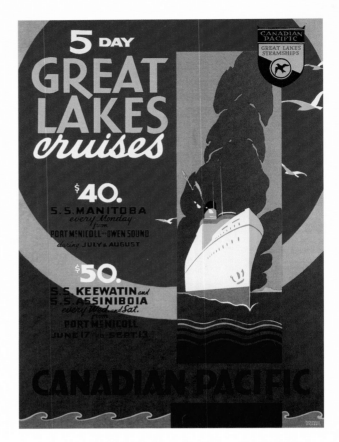

Norman Fraser, 1939; 35 x 48 cm; CP silkscreen No. 495. A6078.

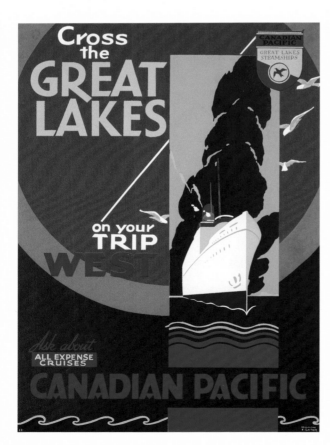

Norman Fraser, 1935; 36 x 49 cm; CP silkscreen No. 221. A6074.

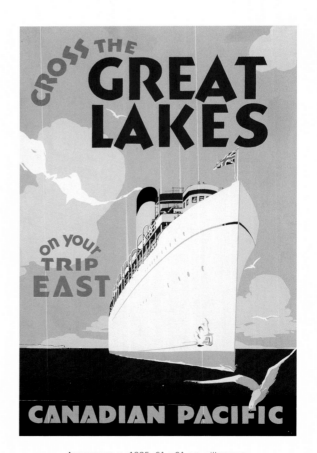

Anonymous, c. 1935; 61 x 91 cm; silkscreen.
UBC-Chung coll. 4014.

Anonymous, c. 1927; 61 x 89 cm; lithograph. A6046.

Anonymous, 1929; 61 x 91 cm; lithograph. Lithographed in Canada. A6048.

Anonymous, c. 1947; 60 x 90 cm; CP silkscreen No. 957. A6379.

Norman Fraser, c. 1935; 37 x 53 cm; CP silkscreen. A6068.

Norman Fraser, c. 1939; 37 x 50 cm; CP silkscreen No. 582. A6077.

St. Lawrence Seaway

9-DAY CRUISES $75 UP

NEW YORK   QUEBEC   MONTREAL

FULL INFORMATION FROM   Canadian Pacific

DUCHESS OF ATHOLL

411

Tom Purvis, 1938; 60 x 90 cm; CP silkscreen No. 411. A6606.

Anonymous, c. 1930; 58 x 93 cm; photolithograph. A6041.

Dudley Ward, 1925; 61 x 100 cm; lithograph. Printed in Canada. UBC-Chung coll. 3934. A6205.

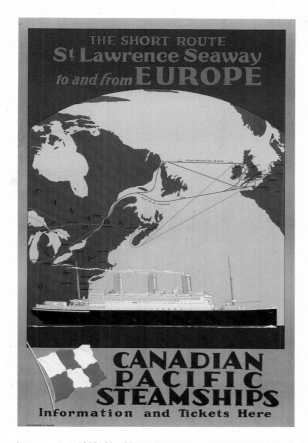

Anonymous, c. 1925; 61 x 91 cm; lithograph. Lithographed in Canada.
McGill University, RBSC.

J.P.G., 1938; 60 x 90 cm; CP silkscreen No. 409. A6374.

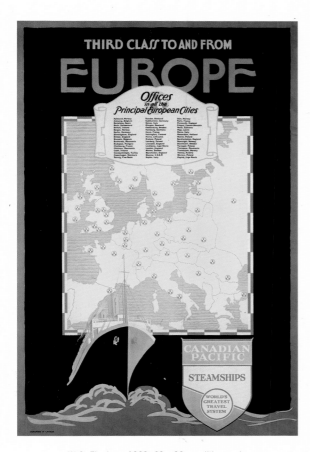

W.C. Finch, c. 1929; 60 x 90 cm; lithograph.
Lithographed in Canada. A6012.

Anonymous, c. 1920; 61 x 100 cm; lithograph. Printed
in Canada. UBC-Chung coll. 3976.

Anonymous, 1924; 63 x 90 cm; lithograph. A6013.

Olive Whitmore, 1930; 62 x 102 cm; lithograph. Printed in
Irish Free State, Cherry & Smallbridge Ltd., Dublin. A6049.

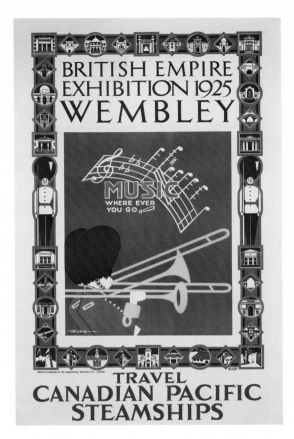

V. Hicks, 1925; 61 x 95 cm; lithograph. Printed in England
by the Dangerfield Printing Co. Ltd., London. A6789.

W.C. Finch, c. 1929; 60 x 90 cm; lithograph.
Lithographed in Canada. A6029.

Charles J. Greenwood, 1929; 56 x 89 cm; lithograph.
Lithographed in Canada. A6183.

Anonymous, c. 1925; 62 x 92 cm; lithograph. Lithographed in Canada. UBC-Chung coll. 3941.

de Forest, 1933; original unknown/reproduced from *The Technique of the Poster,* 1933, p. 160.

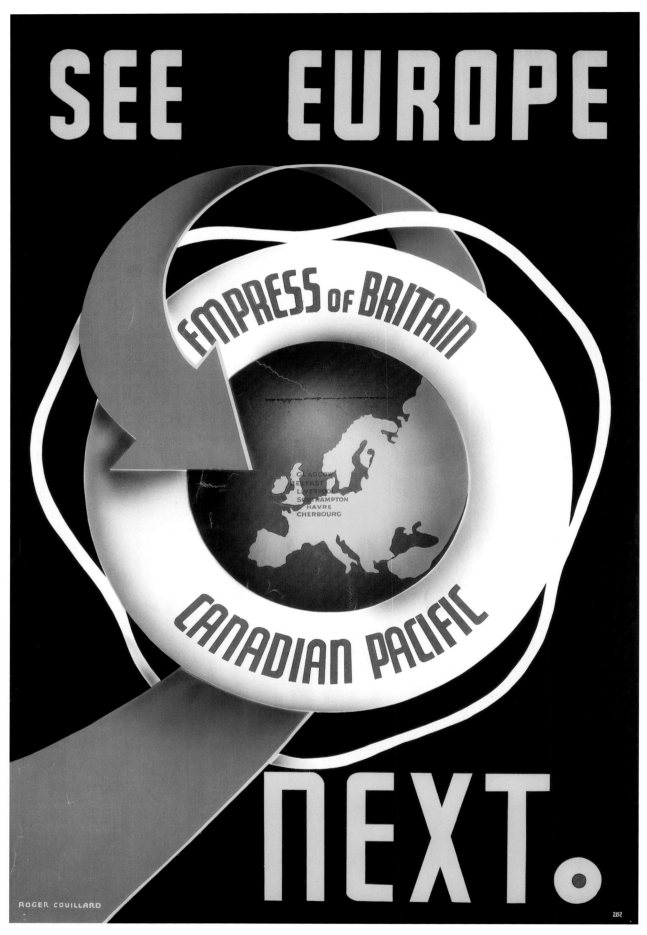

Roger Couillard, 1937; 61 x 91 cm; CP silkscreen. Courtesy of Mrs. Couillard.

Norman Fraser, c. 1935; 60 x 90 cm; CP silkscreen No. 218. A6583.

Norman Fraser, c. 1938; 61 x 91 cm; CP silkscreen No. 479. A6052.

Norman Fraser, 1939; 69 x 91 cm; CP silkscreen No. 509. A6702.

R. Holling, 1924; 60 x 90 cm. Printed in Canada. Courtesy of Library of Congress, Washington, D.C.

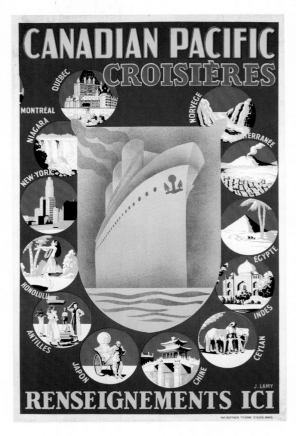

Anonymous, 1923; 60 x 90 cm; lithograph. Printed in U.S.A. A6032.

J. Lamy, c. 1938; 62 x 98 cm; lithograph.
Buttner-Thierry, St-Ouen. A6033.

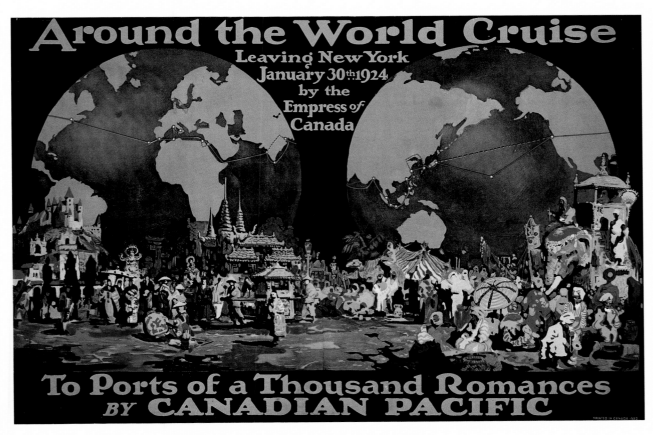

Anonymous, 1923; 90 x 60 cm; lithograph. Printed in Canada. A6037.

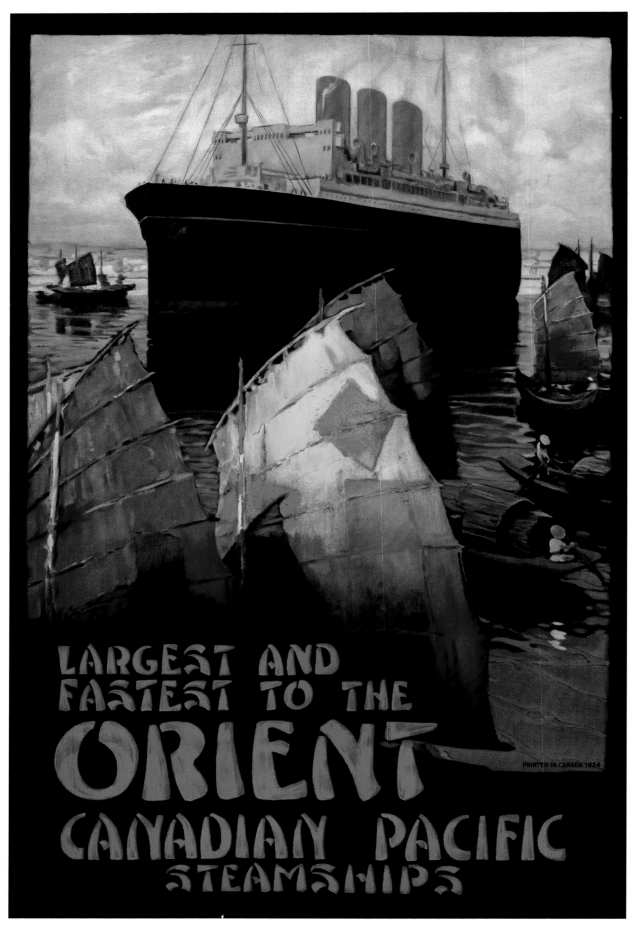

Anonymous, 1924; 61 x 92 cm; lithograph. Printed in Canada. UBC-Chung coll. A6206.

Anonymous, 1923; 63 x 96 cm; lithograph. A6017.

Anonymous, c. 1925; 61 x 92 cm; lithograph. McGill University, RBSC.

A.E. White, 1933; 35 x 69 cm; lithograph. McGill University, RBSC.

These Chinese calendar-posters were probably products of the School
of Shanghai. In the poster on the right, the ship is
the *Empress of Canada*.

Nong, c. 1935; 32 x 89 cm; lithograph. Printed in Hong Kong.
UBC-Chung coll. 3990.

Anonymous, c. 1933; 61 x 91 cm; CP silkscreen No. 135. A6362.

E. Erny, 1929; 62 x 99 cm; lithograph.
Publicité A.V.M. Paris. UBC-Chung coll. 4003.

Percy Angelo Staynes, c. 1932; 59 x 92 cm; lithograph. A6031.

Odin Rosenvinge, c. 1925; 61 x 40 cm; lithograph. Turner and Dunnett, Liverpool. UBC-Chung coll. 3997.

Maurice Logan, c. 1934; 59 x 92 cm; CP silkscreen No. 181. A6582.

Anonymous, c. 1935; 60 x 98 cm; lithograph. A6580.

Maurice Logan, c. 1927; 60 x 90 cm; lithograph.
Lithographed in Canada. A6035.

James C. McKell, c. 1930; 55 x 88 cm; lithograph. A6023.

Anonymous, c. 1935; 62 x 101 cm; silkscreen.
UBC-Chung coll. 3985.

Anonymous, c. 1929; 61 x 92 cm; lithograph. Lithographed in Canada. McGill University, RBSC.

Anonymous, c. 1930; 60 x 98 cm; lithograph. Lithographed in Canada. A6024.

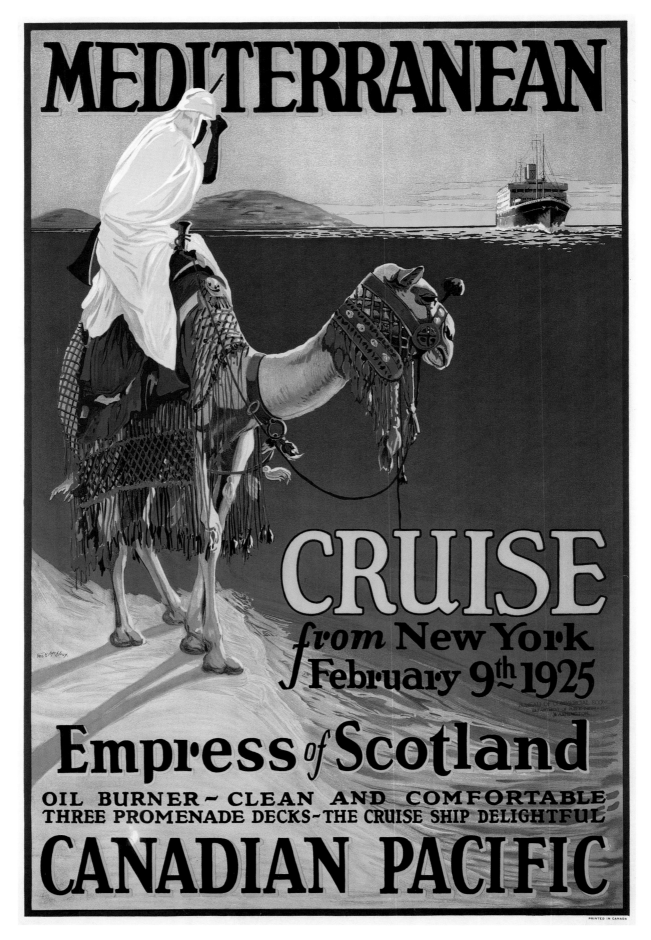

George E. McElroy, 1924; 60 x 90 cm; lithograph. Printed in Canada. Courtesy of Library of Congress, Washington, D.C.

Lendon, c. 1930; 52 x 87 cm; lithograph. A6047.

Anonymous, c. 1937; 61 x 97 cm; photolithograph. Coll. Marc H. Choko.

Anonymous,1936; 37 x 49 cm; silkscreen. A6071.

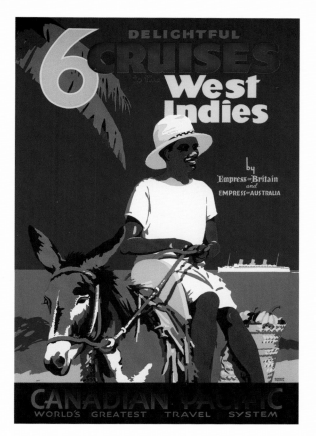

Norman Fraser, c. 1935; 61 x 91 cm; CP silkscreen No. 247. A6588.

Norman Fraser, c. 1934; 45 x 71 cm; CP silkscreen
No. 187. A6599.

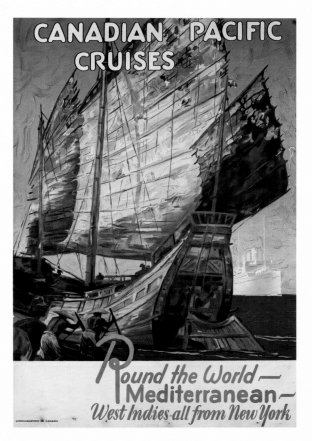

J.C. Valentine, 1925; 60 x 90 cm; lithograph.
Lithographed in Canada. A6045.

Norman Fraser, c. 1938; 60 x 90 cm; silkscreen. A6065.

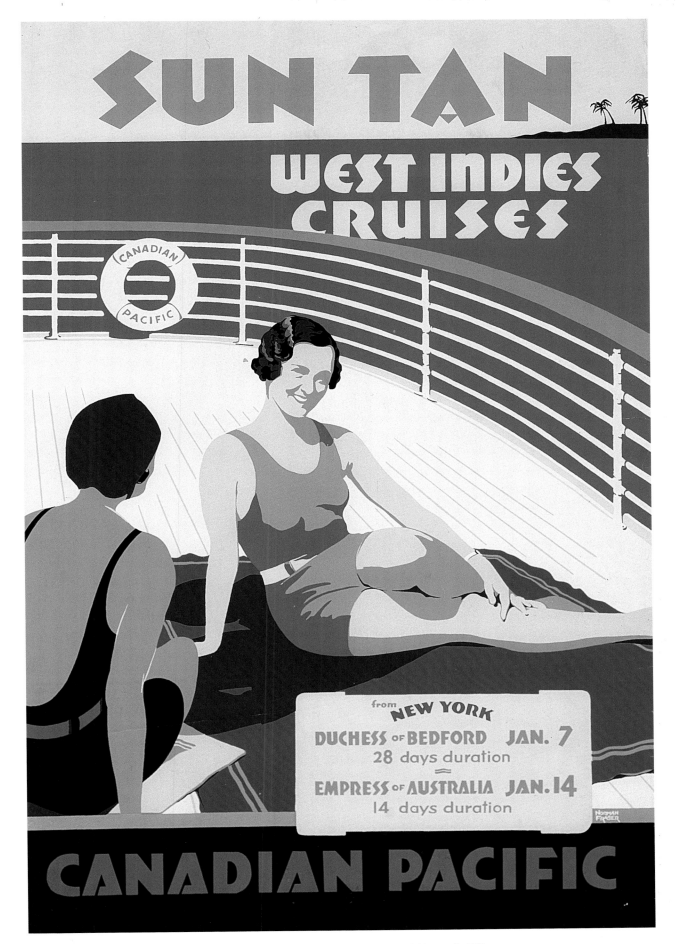

Norman Fraser, c. 1936; 61 x 91 cm; silkscreen. UBC-Chung coll. 4008.

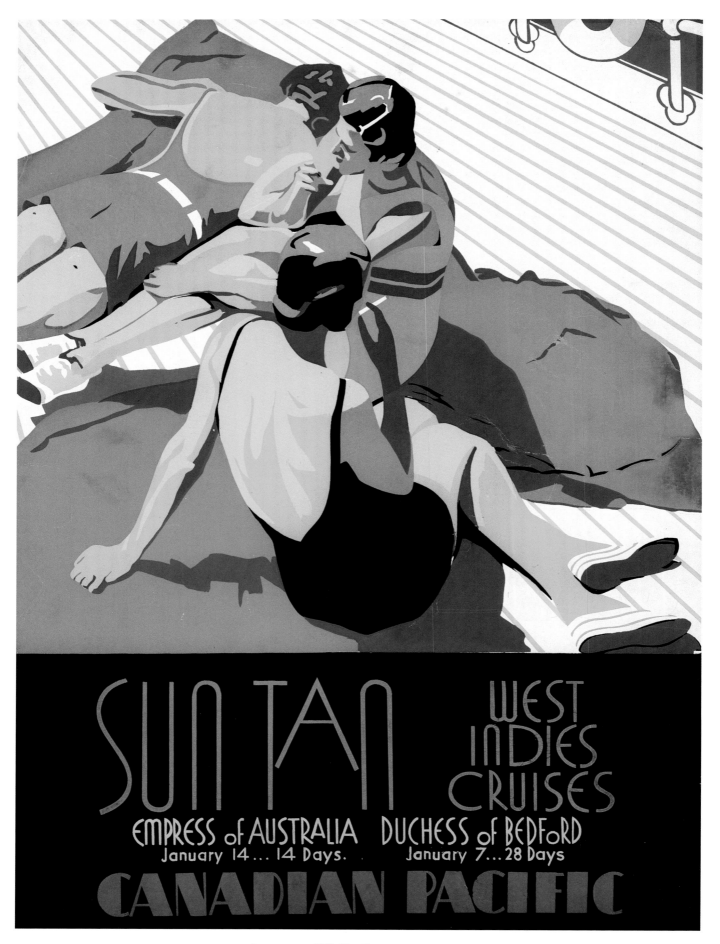

Anonymous, c. 1936; 35 x 48 cm; silkscreen. A6058.

Anonymous, c. 1933; 35 x 48 cm; CP silkscreen No. 144. A6086.

Norman Fraser, c. 1937; 60 x 90 cm; CP silkscreen No. 365. A6604.

Anonymous, c. 1934; 37 x 49 cm; CP silkscreen No. 199. A6083.

Anonymous, 1935; 61 x 91 cm; CP silkscreen No. 239. A6608.

Norman Fraser, 1934; 50 x 72 cm; CP silkscreen No. 176. A6590.

Anonymous, c. 1933; 61 x 90 cm; CP silkscreen No. 134. A6581.

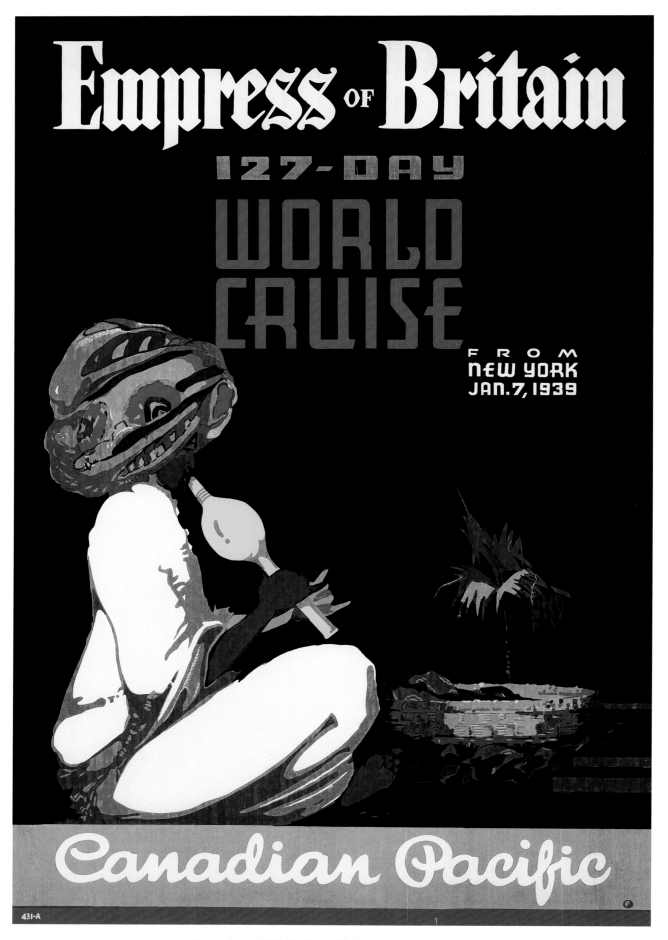

Norman Fraser, 1938; 69 x 91 cm; CP silkscreen No. 431-A. A6593.

The Taj Mahal

VISIT INDIA

W.S. Balitiplis, c. 1936; 63 x 101 cm; lithograph. Printed in India for the Government of India. Bolton Fine Arts Offset Litho., Bombay 7. A6326.

T.F., c. 1926; 60 x 95 cm; lithograph. A6536.

CANADA FOR HOLIDAYS

Vacations in the New World and Old

During the 1920s, a small number of Canadian Pacific posters originated in Canada. Although the quality of the lithography is good, nothing is known about the artists or the printers. The most important phase of poster production in Canada did not begin until 1932, when a silkscreen printing shop was established in the company's Windsor Station headquarters in Montreal.

Under the auspices of the Exhibits Branch of the company's Department of Immigration and Colonization, a fully equipped silkscreen studio was set up, with Ernest W. Scroggie as art director and James Ridge heading the workshop. Scroggie held his post until 1959. Ridge was in charge of the silkscreen studio until he left in 1966. He was replaced by Phil R. Hamilton, who headed the studio until it closed in 1972.

The decision to use serigraphy, or silkscreening, for the majority of posters produced during and after the 1930s was based on practical considerations. As the May 1938 issue of *Canadian Transportation* reported, "The business recession of the early 1930s was the direct reason for the Exhibits Branch entering the field of reproduction." Silkscreening required a significant amount of hand work, which was not a problem during the Depression. The technique did not require any expensive or sophisticated equipment. It was a fast process from conception of the design to final production (preparation was minimal), and modifications to design or text were easily introduced at any stage of the process with little extra cost. Unlike lithography, it required no fragile limestone, expensive metal plates or delicate presses. One needed only a few frames mounted with silk, some type of resin to block off

Tom Purvis, 1938; 60 x 90 cm; lithograph.
S.C. Allen and Co. Ltd., London. A6539.

Charles J. Greenwood, 1938; 51 x 61 cm; CP silkscreen No. 418. A6141.

areas of the screens, paint, an applicator (usually referred to as a squeegee) and paper.

The silkscreen printing technique is based on the stencil technique. It involves stretching finely meshed silk (the silkscreen), upon which a design has been rendered, onto a frame. One screen is required for each colour. The areas to be painted in a particular colour remain open; the remaining area is blocked with resin. By overlapping some of the colours, additional shades may be achieved.

Each frame, in turn, is attached to a base with hinges, ensuring that the successive colours are applied to their precise locations on the final poster. Colour is poured onto the screen at one side and applied evenly across the surface with a squeegee. Hundreds of impressions may thus be made in a relatively short time, and modifications are easy to carry out in mid-production by the removal of a screen, the replacement of a screen or the introduction of a new screen. Blocking of the screens is done by hand or through a photographic process, thus allowing a mixture of techniques and photomontage.

According to the May 1938 issue of *Canadian Transportation*, the first Canadian Pacific posters were printed with a heavy oil paint process in runs of twenty-five copies. Original designs as well as adaptations from lithographic posters were used. This technique was soon abandoned, however, in favour of lighter-textured paints.

Both opaque and transparent colours were used for serigraphic printing during the 1930s and 1940s. In addition to solid colours, the artists and printers experimented with grains, shades and graduated colours. These were obtained by airbrushing parts of the posters or introducing more colour on one side of the squeegee than the other.

By 1940 the poster runs were averaging about 650 copies and often were printed in six or more colours. The serigraphic process was ideal for the company because it made it possible to print a limited number of the same poster economically – allowing for alternate texts for rate, language or destination information.

The graphic designers commissioned to create the poster designs were mainly local freelance commercial artists supplementing their other work. Tom Hall, James Crockart and, above all, Norman Fraser were the most productive artists of the 1930s. They were followed by Roger Couillard, Peter Ewart and others.

The Bow River Valley forms a backdrop for afternoon tea on the terrace of the Banff Springs Hotel.
Date: 1924; Photographer: Brigden's; Source: Canadian Pacific Archives, A28394

Skating has long been a popular winter activity for guests and visitors at the Château Frontenac in Quebec City.
Date: 1946; Photographer: Nicholas Morant (CPR);
Source: Canadian Pacific Archives, M2904

Between the two world wars, CPR's promotional campaigns gave increasing prominence to the concept of vacationing on either side of the Atlantic – depending on where you happened to live. New Canadians were encouraged to visit the Old Country for celebrations, festivals, reunions and commemorations. In Canada the company's ever-expanding chain of hotels meant comfortable lodging not only in the nation's business centres, but also in its sports playgrounds from coast to coast – marvellous destinations for hunting, fishing, mountaineering and cruising the abundant inland lakes, rivers and waterways. "Canada for Holidays," the tourists were told.

The posters for the Algonquin Hotel at St. Andrews-by-the-Sea in New Brunswick invariably featured golfers – all of them women. Although bright colours and summer skies were prominent in the designs, the posters never promised golf "any day of the year" as those for Victoria's Empress Hotel did.

In Quebec City the castlelike Château Frontenac was one of the first great Canadian edifices to be seen by arriving travellers. It soon took on a somewhat iconic role and, for a time, became synonymous with the country in the minds of many. Opened in 1893, the Frontenac acquired its current imposing profile in 1924 with the addition of the large central tower designed by Walter S. Painter. It remains a widely recognized landmark to this day.

The Château Frontenac's historic location on the cliffs above the city and its associations with "Old Quebec" and the hotel's namesake, the governor of New France, were elements the graphic artists were quick to integrate into their designs. As for outdoor pursuits, whereas the Algonquin posters spotlighted golfing, those for the Château and the surrounding area targeted the market for skiing and "Winter Sports in Quebec."

When Toronto's Royal York Hotel opened in 1929, it was heralded as the largest hotel in the British Empire. Its imposing architecture was emphasized in posters, dwarfing everything at street level and backdropped by a dramatic explosion of colour.

CPR western resorts were associated with scenic grandeur. The advertising and poster images often featured views from within the mountain castles, looking out at the beauty of the natural surroundings rather than showcasing the buildings themselves. Once again attractive women are prominent in the foreground, relaxing or sometimes on horseback. In one somewhat bizarre poster

Anonymous, c. 1922; 60 x 90 cm; lithograph. Southam Press Ltd., Montreal. Courtesy of Library of Congress, Washington, D.C.

Opened in 1926, the swimming pool at the Château Lake Louise was the second largest in Canada at that time. The water was obtained from nearby Lake Agnes and warmed to a comfortable 25°C.
Date: 1926; Source: Canadian Pacific Archives, NS17078

by A.C. Leighton for Château Lake Louise, two athletic-looking women, sporting bathing suits and flowing red capes, are perched atop the hotel's diving board. The perspective is such that if they actually dove from the board, they would miss the swimming pool entirely. But the poster has an intriguing decadence about it, and it does show off Lake Louise and the Victoria Glacier.

Two associations – the Sky Line Trail Hikers and the Order of the Trail Riders of the Canadian Rockies – were active in the 1930s. The railway sponsored both groups, which John Murray Gibbon, CPR's publicity man and himself a great raconteur, enthusiastically promoted. The secretary for both groups was based at the CPR's Windsor Station headquarters in Montreal. Typically, small outings were organized whenever a few members felt so inspired. An annual and well-publicized hike or ride featured a few local poets, singing cowboys and other colourful characters to keep the groups entertained around the evening campfires.

Alfred Crocker Leighton, c. 1938; 60 x 90 cm; CP silkscreen No. 398. A6358.

Norman Fraser, c. 1938; 30 x 48 cm; silkscreen. A6124.

At times, in the few tourist areas where CPR could not offer the comforts of its own hostelries, the company entered into partnerships with other operators. One poster for the Bon Echo Inn on the Mazinawe Lakes near Kaladar, Ontario – executed by Group of Seven artist A.Y. Jackson – reassured travellers they could reach their hotel via the Canadian Pacific Railway. Once there they would find "good fishing, boating & other outdoor sports."

Like the golf and ski posters, the hunting and fishing posters of the twenties, thirties and early forties are visually dramatic. They feature simple messages and bold typefaces, along with large, colourful images of sportsmen in action or graphic depictions of the fish and game they pursued.

As E.T. Noltie, director of exhibits for CPR's Department of Immigration, said, "The message should be quickly read by the passing public, particularly in the poster and show-card end of the business … our aim there being to make these reproductions colourfully dramatic, yet simple in conception, so that the message may be readily grasped."

The lobby of the Banff Springs Hotel as it appeared before the rebuilding of the north wing and enlargement of the central Painter Tower during the winter of 1926–27.
Date: 1924; Photographer: Brigden's; Source: Canadian Pacific Archives, A28374

A new style of rail service was developed in the 1920s. The *Trans-Canada Limited* train offered a virtual land cruise across the country. Rather than providing a long trip in coach seats, the "limited" status of this service ensured that all were well ensconced in sleeping cars, with rolling amenities that included lounge, dining and observation cars. Publicists called it the "Fastest Train on the Continent." Typically, *Trans-Canada Limited* posters featured diminutive red CPR trains in dramatically lit alpine settings, accentuating the majesty of the CPR's route through what the company liked to call "the Canadian Pacific Rockies."

"Safety, Comfort, and Economy" were, as the ads said, the benefits of "Travel by Train." And "for Greater Comfort," read one sign, "when traveling at night, take a section – upper and lower berth – at a very nominal charge."

The poster designs accentuated elegance, style and even a subtle nobility, as suggested by the deco-style "Travel Canadian Pacific" poster that shows a sophisticated female rail passenger in the foreground, backed by the looming streamlined *Royal Hudson* locomotive 2850. That renowned engine, not coincidentally, played a starring role in the 1939 Canadian royal tour of King George VI and Queen Elizabeth. It was the first locomotive of its class to bear royal crown castings on its running boards.

Hal Ross Perrigard, 1923; 60 x 90 cm; lithograph. Printed in Canada. A6792.

In the 1930s Canadian Pacific decided to enter the airline business. With the formation of the government-operated Trans-Canada Airlines in 1936, however, this venture was postponed. Then, in 1937, the CPR introduced its first diesel-electric locomotive, heralding the most significant change to occur in the history of railroading – the phasing out of steam locomotives like the *Royal Hudson* in favour of diesel locomotives.

E.T. Noltie explained the philosophy of the Exhibits Branch during this period in the company's history: "Canada has been called 'a land of magnificent distances,'" he said. "It is vital, therefore, from a Canadian Pacific transportation point of view that knowledge of certain parts of the country should be conveyed in a vivid and interesting way to residents of other parts, if travel is to be consistently and persistently stimulated." This strategy was echoed in the ads inviting the public to "Ask Canadian Pacific about Canada."

In 1939 King George VI and Queen Elizabeth arrived at Quebec City on the CP liner *Empress of Australia*. The royal party then embarked upon a coast-to-coast tour aboard a special train.
Date: 1939; Source: Canadian Pacific Archives, A15194

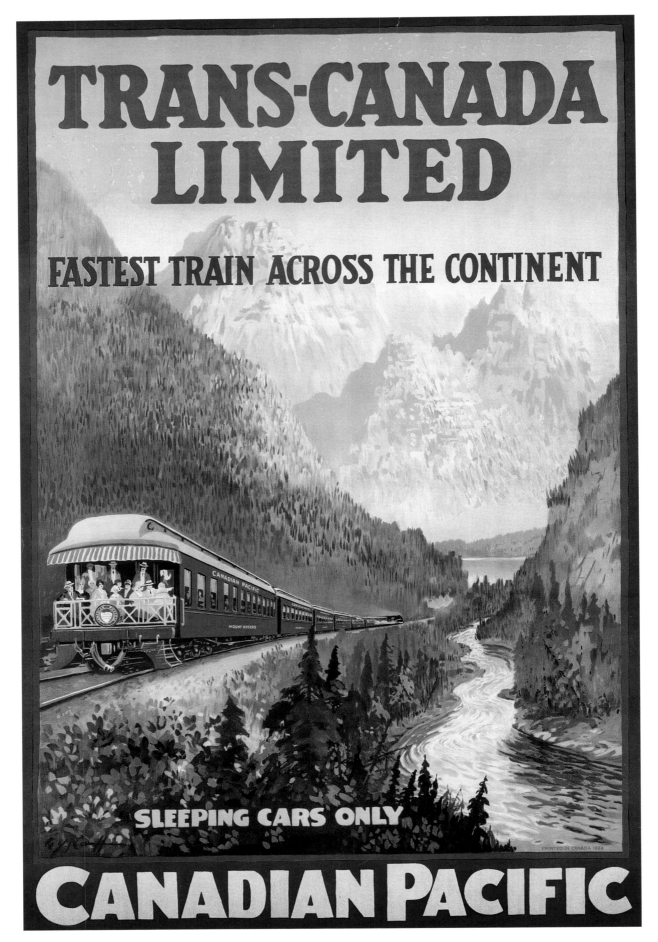

G.Y. Kauffman, 1924; 60 x 90 cm; lithograph. Printed in Canada. A6350.

Gordon Fraser Gillespie, 1925; 60 x 90 cm; lithograph. Printed in Canada. A6400.

Norman Fraser, 1937; 60 x 90 cm; CP silkscreen No. 343. A6365.

Peter Ewart, 1942; 60 x 90 cm; CP silkscreen No. 692. Coll. David L. Jones.

Wilfred Langdon Kihn, c. 1925; lithograph. Lithographed in Canada. McGill University, RBSC.

Based on design by Wilfred Langdon Kihn, c. 1946; 60 x 90 cm;
CP silkscreen No. 885. A6546.

Morley Rigal, 1933; 56 x 92 cm; CP silkscreen No. 168. A6521.

Anonymous, 1939; 36 x 50 cm; CP silkscreen No. 516. A6143.

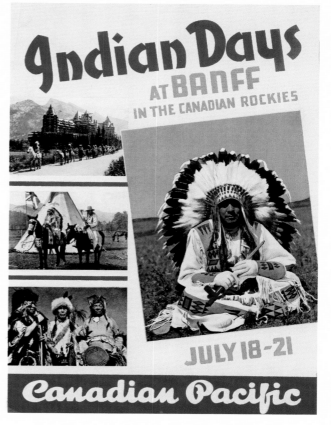

Anonymous, c. 1937; 37 x 50 cm; silkscreen. A6144.

Anonymous, c. 1932; 60 x 90 cm; CP silkscreen (heavy ink). Courtesy of the Astrolabe Gallery, Ottawa.

James C. McKell, c. 1932; 61 x 91 cm; CP silkscreen (heavy ink). A6512.

James Crockart, 1936; 60 x 90 cm; lithograph. A6189.

Kenneth Shoesmith, c. 1930; 60 x 90 cm; lithograph.
S.C. Allen and Co., London. A6191.

Trumpf, c. 1935; 61 x 91 cm; lithograph. McGill University, RBSC.

Anonymous, c. 1939; 60 x 90 cm; lithograph.
Southam Press. A6357.

Anonymous, c. 1940; 62 x 97 cm; photolithograph.
Courtesy of The Astrolabe Gallery, Ottawa.

Peter Ewart, c. 1941; 61 x 92 cm; CP silkscreen No. 645. A6508.

Norman Fraser, c. 1939; 35 x 48 cm; CP silkscreen No. 536. A6540.

Norman Fraser, c. 1936; 35 x 48 cm; CP silkscreen No. 257. A6127.

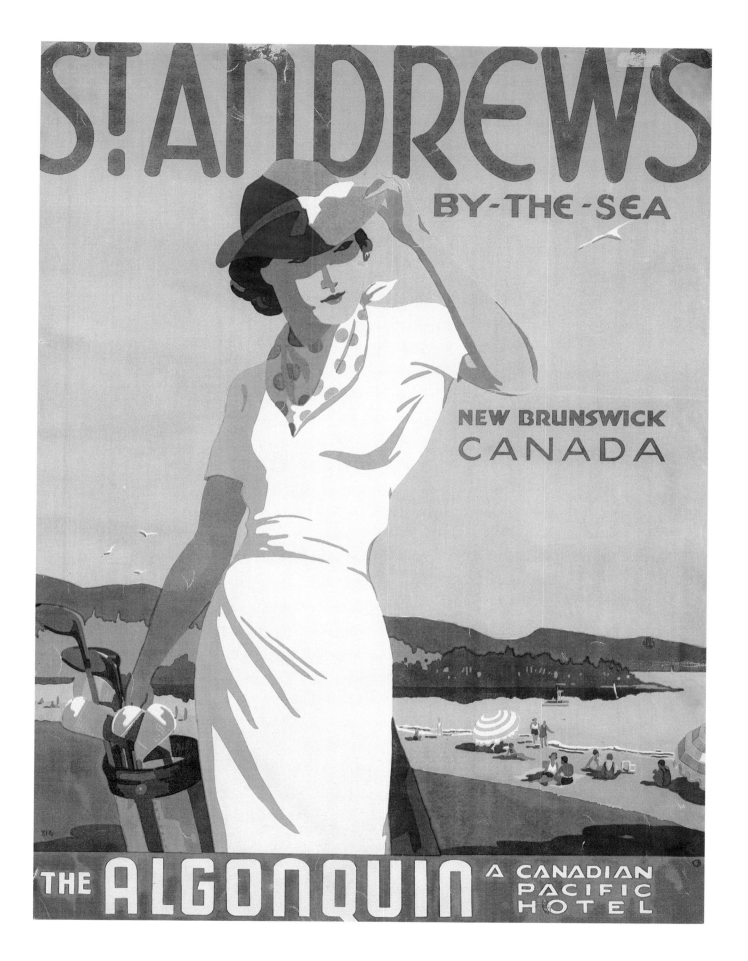

Norman Fraser, 1937; 37 x 50 cm; CP silkscreen. A6126.

Norman Fraser, 1934; 46 x 72 cm; CP silkscreen No. 195. A6505.

Norman Fraser, c. 1939; 63 x 95 cm; CP silkscreen. A6626.

E., 1929; 60 x 90 cm; lithograph. Printed in Canada. A6192.

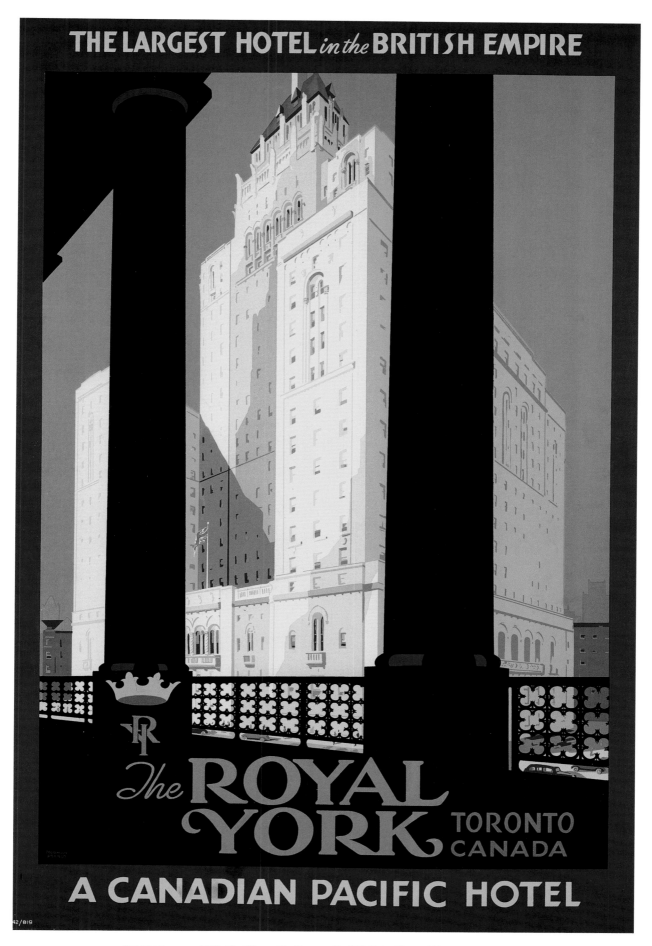

Norman Fraser, c. 1946; 60 x 90 cm; CP silkscreen No. 819 (1st edition c. 1935, No. 242). A6356.

Anonymous, c. 1933; 60 x 90 cm; CP silkscreen. A6121.

R.H. Palenske, 1929; lithograph. Stovel Co. Ltd., Winnipeg, Canada.
A6187.

Anonymous, c. 1930; 55 x 70 cm; lithograph. Lithographed in Canada.
A6264.

Anonymous, c. 1930; 60 x 91 cm; lithograph. A6184.

Anonymous, c. 1939; 62 x 92 cm; CP silkscreen No. 560. A6709.

Anonymous, 1924; 60 x 90 cm; lithograph.
Printed in Canada. A6185.

James Crockart, 1950; 60 x 90 cm; lithograph.
Lithographed in Canada. A6618.

Norman Fraser, c. 1939; 61 x 91 cm; CP silkscreen. A6545.

Anonymous, c. 1939; 61 x 91 cm; CP silkscreen. A6768.

Peter Ewart, c. 1947; 60 x 90 cm; CP silkscreen. Courtesy of Suntory Museum, Osaka.

A.Y. Jackson, 1924; 41 x 59 cm; silkscreen. UBC-Chung coll. 4032.

After Thomas Hall, c. 1939; 60 x 90 cm; CP silkscreen No. 578. A6695.

Anonymous, c. 1939; 60 x 90 cm; CP silkscreen No. 594. A6696.

Thomas Hall, c. 1939; CP silkscreen No. 534. A6692.

Carl Burger, 1939; 60 x 91 cm; CP silkscreen No. 490. A6364.

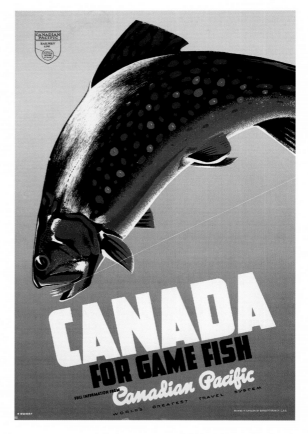

Peter Ewart, 1942; 61 x 91 cm; CP silkscreen No. 702.
Printed in Canada by Exhibits Branch, CPR. A6683.

Thomas Hall, 1938; 60 x 90 cm; CP silkscreen No. 437. A6542.

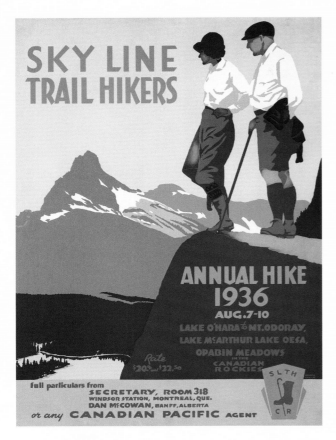

Norman Fraser, 1936; 37 x 50 cm; CP silkscreen. A6776.

Charles J. Greenwood, c. 1938; 36 x 49 cm; CP silkscreen
No. 414. A6171.

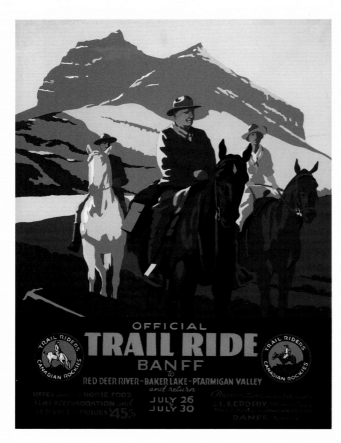

Norman Fraser, c. 1935; 36 x 49 cm; CP silkscreen No. 213. A6164.

Anonymous, 1939; 51 x 61 cm; CP silkscreen No. 497. A6161.

Norman Fraser, 1935; 35 x 48 cm; CP silkscreen No. 214. A6122.

WINTER SPORTS IN QUEBEC

Centering round the Chateau Frontenac

Triple-Chute Toboggan Slide
on Dufferin Terrace

Skating and Curling Rinks

Ski-jump on Citadel Hill, all in connection with the Hotel

HOCKEY AND CURLING MATCHES

Cross-country Ski-ing and Snow-shoe Tramps

Ski-joring and Attractive Sleigh Drives through beautiful and historic country

CANADIAN PACIFIC RAILWAY

Anonymous, c. 1925; 60 x 90 cm; lithograph. McGill University, RBSC.

Anonymous, c. 1927; 60 x 91 cm; lithograph. A6622.

Anonymous, c. 1934; 36 x 49 cm; CP silkscreen No. 192. A6132.

John Vickery, c. 1938; 66 x 91 cm; CP silkscreen. A6511.

Thomas Hall, c. 1937; 62 x 92 cm; CP silkscreen. A6646.

Norman Fraser, c. 1936; 36 x 49 cm; CP silkscreen. A6136.

Norman Fraser, c. 1936; 37 x 52 cm; CP silkscreen No. 248. A6130.

Thomas Hall, c. 1938; 37 x 49 cm; CP silkscreen. A6131.

Norman Fraser, 1937; 37 x 50 cm; CP silkscreen No. 300. A6134.

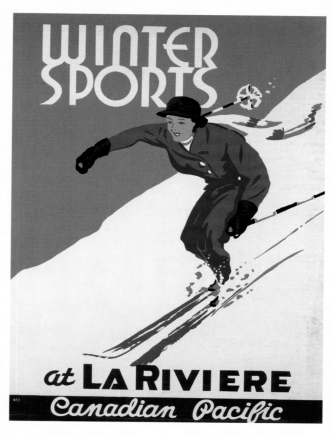

Norman Fraser, c. 1938; 37 x 50 cm; CP silkscreen No. 460. A6133.

John Vickery, c. 1937; 61 x 92 cm; CP silkscreen No. 360. A6518.

John Vickery, 1937; 61 x 91 cm; CP silkscreen P472. A6516.

Anonymous, c. 1939; 61 x 91 cm; CP silkscreen No. 543. Printed in Canada by Exhibits Branch, CPR. A6515.

Anonymous, c. 1939; 61 x 91 cm; CP silkscreen No. 544. A6506.

Anonymous, c. 1939; 37 x 50 cm; CP silkscreen. A6129.

Anonymous, 1945; 60 x 90 cm; silkscreen. A6502.

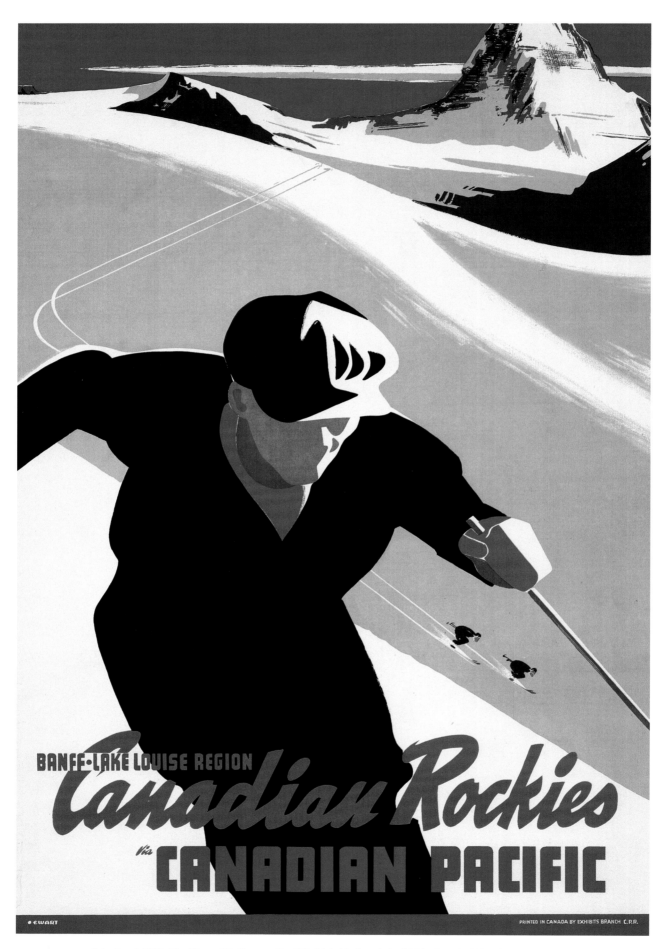

Peter Ewart, 1941; 60 x 90 cm; CP silkscreen No. 679. Printed in Canada by Exhibits Branch, CPR. A6147, 6501, 6535.

Peter Ewart, c. 1941; 61 x 91 cm; CP silkscreen No. 678. A6541.

CANADIAN PACIFIC
ON THE JOB

ROLLING TOWARDS VICTORY

Fifty thousand railway men and women daily guard and speed half a million wheels over twenty thousand miles of track in the Canadian Pacific war effort

Norman Fraser, 1941; 58 x 88 cm; CP silkscreen No. 618. A6786.

ROLLING TOWARDS VICTORY

On the job during the war years

Canadian Pacific made a valuable contribution to Canada's efforts in both world wars. While the railway line was an essential means of conveying men and materiel to Canada's ocean ports, the company's steamships played a similar role in moving them to the theatres of war in Europe and, in the Second World War, Southeast Asia.

With the start of the First World War, the company's resources were placed at the disposal of the Canadian government and the British Empire. Many of its largest and fastest ships were requisitioned by the British Admiralty. Fourteen of them were lost in the performance of their duty, a sacrifice that was unmatched by any other merchant shipping fleet during the war. Overall, millions of troops and passengers, plus approximately four million tons of cargo, were transported.

A skeleton service was maintained on both the Atlantic and the Pacific during the conflict, but advertising was kept to a minimum. While the Canadian government turned out hundreds of posters recruiting men, selling bonds and encouraging the conservation of vital resources and supplies, Canadian Pacific, which was not yet operating its own printing studio, did not issue any posters of its own design. By the Second World War, however, the company's Exhibits Branch geared up for the challenge and turned out a number of simple but effective posters.

When war struck again in 1939, Canadian Pacific was involved at once. On land, more than 300 million tons of freight and 86 million passengers were transported by train. At sea, twenty-two ships steamed more than three million miles in the service of the British Admiralty while

During the Second World War, CPR's Angus Shops in Montreal produced 1,400 of these "Valentine" army tanks for shipment to Russia to assist in their drive to force the German army out of eastern Europe. Date: 1941–1943; Photographer: CPR; Source: Canadian Pacific Archives, NS.3004

The *Princess Marguerite* of the CPR's British Columbia Coastal Steamship Service sank in the Mediterranean after being struck by a German torpedo while transporting troops from Port Said to Cyprus. Date: August 17, 1942; Source: Canadian Pacific Archives, NS. 863

carrying almost one million passengers. The company's mechanical department built munitions, anti-aircraft guns, marine engines and tanks. In light of its experience in the air business – in 1942 ten small regional airlines had been consolidated to form Canadian Pacific Air Lines – Canadian Pacific was also called upon to organize and operate six air observer schools to train navigators. In addition, the company operated a bomber delivery service, flying Canadian-built planes to Britain. It formed the basis of the Royal Air Force Ferry Command.

As the war progressed, Canadian Pacific periodically printed posters announcing the number of employees who had enlisted in the armed forces. Graphic considerations were not as important as the raw impact of the impressive statistics listed in boldface type. By August 31, 1945, nearly one-quarter of the company's personnel, more than twenty thousand individuals, had volunteered for active service.

"Canadian Pacific – On the Job" was the proud claim of a bold company war poster showing a head-on view of a steam locomotive, flanked on one side by a troop train and on the other by a train moving tanks and war materiel. This time the emphasis was on the home guard of "fifty thousand railway men and women" who "daily guard and speed half a million wheels over twenty thousand miles of track in the Canadian Pacific war effort."

In keeping with a nationwide campaign to ration raw materials of importance to the war machine, Canadian Pacific made every effort to minimize the use of these items and appealed to its employees and the travelling public to do the same. Hundreds of government posters in stations, hotels and offices implored Canadians to "Save Rubber," "Save Tin," "Save Rags," and "Don't Waste Coal."

The railway's mechanical department worked in three shifts daily, extending the working life of the engines and cars and supplementing routine work with munitions production. The company shops turned out heavy artillery shells, entire anti-aircraft guns, marine engines and fully operational Valentine tanks. These tanks, mostly used in eastern Europe, were claimed by the Russians to have "proved themselves the best of all our imported tanks."

In order to help illustrate the resolve of Russian allies, a selection of Soviet war posters was brought to Canada for exhibition in the company's Montreal headquarters. The originals, with printed inscriptions in Russian, were displayed with English translations. Slogans like "The dirty Nazi pest – we'll destroy without a rest" and "Hit the

Peter Ewart, 1942; 60 x 90 cm; CP silkscreen No. 718. A6207.

enemy right in his nest" demonstrated the determination of the Russian resistance.

Victory Bond campaigns were wholeheartedly supported by Canadian Pacific. D.C. Coleman, who had become company president in 1943, decided to issue a poster with a photograph of himself and an appeal to employees. The text read:

I am confident that Canadian Pacific men and women will maintain their proud record by generously responding to the call to buy Canada's Fifth Victory Loan Bonds, and thus again support the magnificent war effort of more than 17,000 Company people and all other Canadians on Active Service at Home and Abroad.

D.C. Coleman
Chairman and President
Canadian Pacific Railway Company

Anonymous, c. 1939; 71 x 55 cm; lithograph. UBC-Chung coll. 3906.

Printed by the Exhibits Branch in red, white and blue, these posters were distributed widely across the CPR system. In addition, the concourse of Windsor Station, where thousands of passengers passed through daily, displayed two billboard-sized posters promoting the sale of war savings certificates.

Canadian Pacific employees organized their own campaign in support of the war effort. Known as the "Golden Bomber Fund," the promotion solicited all kinds of gold items to help finance the purchase of aircraft for the Allies. A shiny gold and dark blue poster was printed to deliver the message: "Give Your Old Gold." Watches, rings, bracelets, walking-stick heads, souvenir coins, championship medals, lodge emblems – even dental plates and solid nuggets – were collected and used to procure two Spitfires for the Royal Air Force.

Safety and efficiency became themes of great importance. The consequences of negligence were clearly conveyed in a poster showing what could happen to a locomotive through a few moments of inattention or carelessness. "In less than a minute – this became this" was illustrated by a powerful locomotive and the same machine lying in ruins.

Other posters highlighted travel situations with cartoons and advised how best to avoid entanglements and inconveniences. Canadian travel and vacation activities,

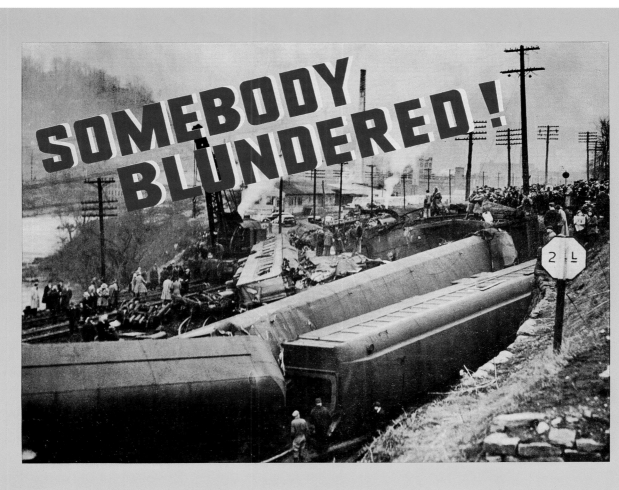

Don't be the Monkey Wrench that causes something like this !

Anonymous, 1943; 61 x 91 cm; CP silkscreen No. 744. A6784.

Anonymous, 1942; 60 x 90 cm; CP silkscreen No. 722. A6760.

particularly skiing, continued to be promoted in the United States and, although not many poster designs were introduced during the war years, the company's offices continued its window displays.

The successful conclusion of the war called for a special poster to celebrate the return to business as usual. The announcement "The Seas Are Free Again" appeared beneath a Canadian Pacific house flag on an open expanse of calm, peaceful water.

Members of one of Canadian Pacific's Air Raid Precaution units stage a mobile display of their contribution to civil defence.
Date: c.1941; Source: Canadian Pacific Archives, WAR.75.2

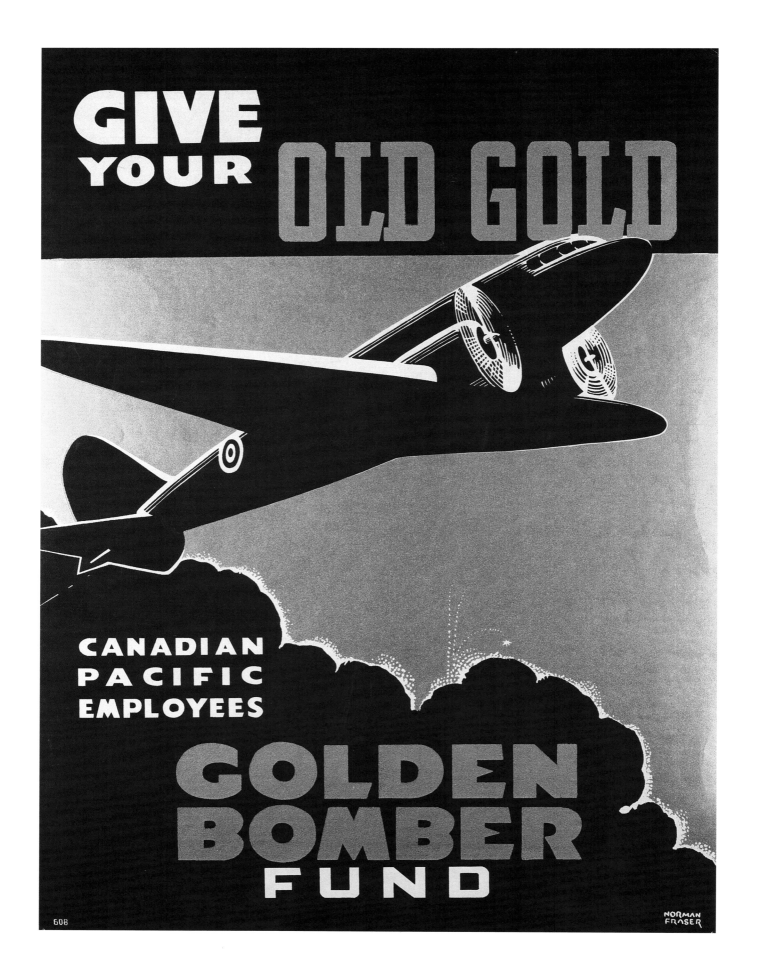

Norman Fraser, c. 1940; 35 x 48 cm; CP silkscreen No. 604. A6329.

Bomber Crew

Train Crew

THEIR LIVES AND THE SUCCESS OF THEIR JOBS DEPEND ON TEAM WORK

Anonymous, c. 1943; original unknown. NS 4578.

Norman Fraser, 1942; 61 x 93 cm; CP silkscreen No. 705.
Printed in Canada by Exhibits Branch, CPR. A6708.

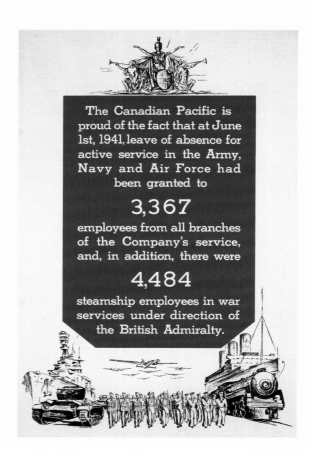

Anonymous, 1941; 60 x 90 cm; CP silkscreen. A6680.

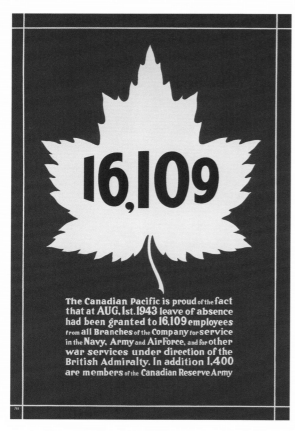

Anonymous, 1943; 61 x 92 cm; CP silkscreen No. 785. A6547.

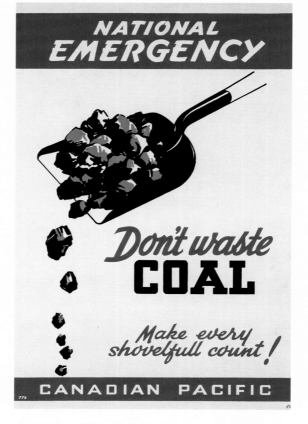

Norman Fraser, 1943; 60 x 90 cm; CP silkscreen No. 774. A6713.

Peter Ewart, 1943; 60 x 90 cm; CP silkscreen No. 739. A6714.

Anonymous, c. 1943; 37 x 50 cm; CP silkscreen No. 735. A6253.

Anonymous, c. 1943; 37 x 50 cm; CP silkscreen. A6656.

Anonymous, 1943; 37 x 50 cm; CP silkscreen. A6255.

Anonymous, 1943; 37 x 50 cm; CP silkscreen No. 756B. A6254.

THE SEAS ARE FREE AGAIN...

Canadian Pacific ships carried men and machines to war.....
Now, they move the Service personnel home, victorious.
Soon they will serve you again in peacetime travel and trade

Meantime, inquire here for overseas travel regulations.

Canadian Pacific Steamships

Anonymous, 1946; 61 x 92 cm; CP silkscreen No. 856. A6788.

Roger Couillard, 1950; 60 x 90 cm; CP silkscreen. Printed in Canada. Coll. Marc H. Choko.

CANADIAN PACIFIC SPANS THE WORLD AGAIN

Tourism in the postwar era

After the Second World War, Canadian Pacific's Department of Immigration and Colonization was dissolved, but the Exhibits Branch continued to operate as a division of the company's Public Relations Department (now Corporate Communications and Public Affairs).

Poster production centred on three main subjects: the return of scheduled steamship service to the Atlantic; the introduction of the new transcontinental passenger train, *The Canadian;* and the expansion of Canadian Pacific's airline service into a transcontinental and intercontinental carrier.

Postwar steamship posters can be readily identified by the Canadian Pacific red-and-white-checkered house flags painted on the sides of the ships' funnels. The poster "Sail White Empress to Europe" is a good example of the attempt to recapture the grandeur of the golden era of the 1930s by emulating classic poster design techniques. Only the funnels place it squarely in the 1950s.

On the rails, the largest steam locomotives to be built for the CPR made impressive subjects for the graphic artists. A massive Selkirk locomotive emerging from a mountain tunnel, trailing a series of white lines to indicate speed, was featured on an "Across Canada" poster. A similar rendition of diesel locomotive 4040 illustrates the final transition from the steam to diesel era that took place during the 1950s.

No postwar railway development, however, received as much public attention as the brief renaissance in passenger train service brought about by Canadian Pacific Railway's *The Canadian,* in direct competition with Canadian National Railways' *Supercontinental.*

A typical Canadian Pacific Railway Co. window display in the 1940s and 1950s.

Date: 1948; Source: Canadian Pacific Archives, A29589

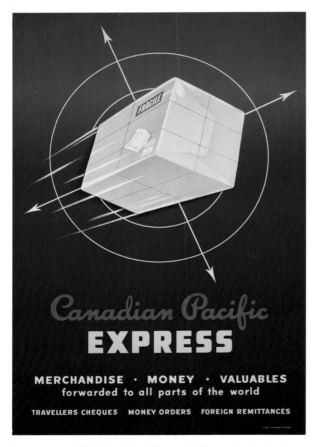

Anonymous, c. 1951; 61 x 92 cm; lithograph. Lithographed in Canada. A6783.

Inaugurated April 15, 1955, *The Canadian* presented a new look in Canadian railway trains with its stainless-steel coaches, scenic domes and streamlined contours.

Amidst a flurry of newspaper and magazine advertisements, flyers, pamphlets and brochures, many of the posters for *The Canadian* were a throwback to the heyday of the *Trans-Canada Limited,* favouring mountain backdrops to showcase the longest scenic-dome train ride in the world.

But the days of commercial rail travel were numbered, and increasingly the major thrust of the company's advertising campaigns was directed toward the expanding airline business. From a northern bush service the airline grew into a national and intercontinental carrier, operating major routes to Europe, South America and Southeast Asia. Advertising began in earnest during the war to promote the "Wings of the World's Greatest Travel System." Very early air service posters feature Lockheed Lodestars, two of which were allocated to Canadian Pacific Air Lines by the postwar U.S. joint chiefs of staff as war reparations.

On July 13, 1949, flights from Vancouver to Sydney, Australia, were inaugurated on Canadair-Four aircraft. Their engines had proven themselves reliable in fighter aircraft during the war. Some of the poster designs for the biweekly, fifteen-hour flights to Australia featured the aircraft's pressurized cabins, by now a requirement of high-altitude flights but nevertheless something to bring to the travelling public's attention. Weekly service to Tokyo and Hong Kong began September 19, 1949, also on Canadair-Fours.

During the 1950s Canadian Pacific extended its network to South America and Europe, mostly using the first truly intercontinental aircraft, the DC-6. Honolulu, Lima and Mexico City became destinations in 1953. The Lima route was extended to Buenos Aires in 1956 and Santiago was added the following year, but the biggest prize was winning an air route across the Atlantic.

"Europe," announced a poster in big bold letters when Canadian Pacific was authorized to begin scheduled flights to Amsterdam in 1955. The addition of coloured "northern lights" to the design was a subtle reminder that the adopted polar route was the most direct line to the continent. Two years later, when Madrid and Lisbon were added to the company's overseas routes, matadors and bathing beauties were included in the posters to entice transatlantic fliers.

Amid the many successes of the growing airline business, one poster stands out as a poignant footnote to a tragic experience with jet aircraft. In 1949, two of the experimental de Havilland Comets were ordered by Canadian Pacific Air Lines. The first was received for test flights in 1953. On March 3 that year, while on a trial run in the South Pacific, a Comet christened *Empress of Hawaii* crashed as it took off from Karachi, Pakistan, killing all on board. A poster, prepared and printed in advance of the inaugural flight, advertises an "Across the Pacific" service that did not materialize. The accident was a serious setback for the company's plans to convert to jet aircraft, and it was a full decade before DC-8s were flying on most of Canadian Pacific's routes.

After the war, the increased use of offset lithography, which allowed thousands of large-format posters to be printed rapidly at low cost, slowed down the production of serigraphic posters. Many designs were once again handed to outside printers. Most of the posters for Canadian Pacific Air Lines were produced by printers in Vancouver, with a series printed in England. Nevertheless, Canadian Pacific's silkscreen studio remained active. For runs of one thousand or less, serigraphy remained a competitive technique.

In 1968 the company adopted a new symbol, called the "multimark," and its divisions were given new modal names: CP Rail, CP Ships, CP Air, CP Express, CP Transport. By 1971 the name Canadian Pacific Railway Company was no longer appropriate for the varied operations of the organization and was changed to Canadian Pacific Limited.

The silkscreen studio was not closed down entirely until 1972. During the period between 1883 and that date, the company turned out more than 2,500 posters, including more than 1,000 of its own designs featuring the work of Canadian artists, a production that may well be unrivalled by any other company.

Most of the posters in this book have been selected from the approximately seven hundred posters in the Canadian Pacific Railway Archives. About thirty others are from the exceptional private collection of Dr. Wally Chung, which is now housed in the University of British Columbia Rare Books and Special Collections. CP posters can also be found at McGill University's Rare Books and Special Collections in Montreal, at the National Archives in Ottawa and at the Library of Congress in Washington.

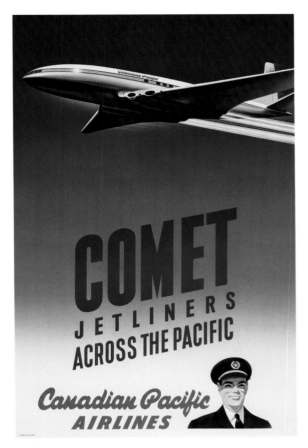

Peter Ewart, 1952; 60 x 90 cm; lithograph. Lithographed in Canada. McGill University, RBSC. A6531.

181

From time to time, CP posters also pop up at auctions around the world. As strange as it may seem, it is easier to find these now rare posters in the United States or Europe than in Canada. In both the United States and Europe, Canadian Pacific posters have been better valued, preserved and collected than they have been in Canada.

Although poster art maintained a tenuous foothold well into the jet age, photography was becoming prevalent in advertising. It was only a matter of time before photographic designs replaced the graphic interpretations that had delighted the public for decades. And while it may be said that a picture is worth a thousand words, rarely can a photograph deliver a message in a flash, or leave a lasting and favourable impression, as could the best posters executed by the graphic artists of the CPR.

Peter Ewart, c. 1946; 76 x 102 cm; CP silkscreen No. 910. A6176.

Canadian Pacific
WORLD'S GREATEST TRAVEL SYSTEM
RAILWAYS, STEAMSHIPS, AIRLINES, HOTELS, COMMUNICATIONS, EXPRESS

Roger Couillard, c. 1954; 62 x 92 cm; serigraph CP No. 1480. Coll. UBC-Chung. 4108.

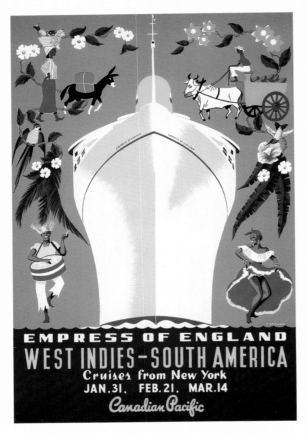

Roger Couillard, c. 1958; 60 x 90 cm; silkscreen. ANC 137956.

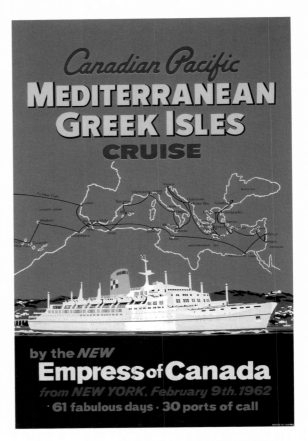

Anonymous, c. 1962; 61 x 91 cm; silkscreen. Printed in Canada.
UBC-Chung coll. 3948.

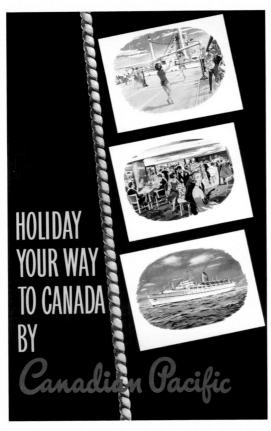

Anonymous, c. 1962; 63 x 101 cm; lithograph.
Coll. Marc H. Choko.

Anonymous, 1946; 61 x 92 cm; CP silkscreen No. 908. A6001.

Roger Couillard, c. 1956; 60 x 90 cm; CP silkscreen No. 1726. ANC 137963.

Anonymous, c. 1963; 60 x 90 cm; lithograph. A6337.

Anonymous, c. 1963; 60 x 90 cm; photolithograph. A6336.

Anonymous, 1961; 61 x 92 cm; photolithograph. Printed in Canada.
A6003.

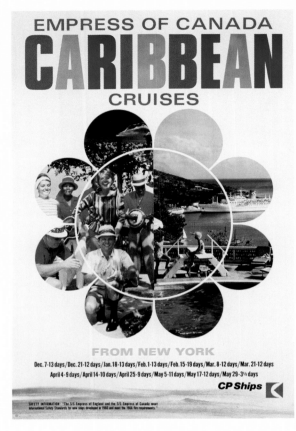

Anonymous, c. 1968; 60 x 90 cm; photolithograph. A6006.

Anonymous, c. 1963; 60 x 90 cm; photolithograph. A6007.

Anonymous, 1969; 60 x 90 cm; photolithograph. A6005.

Roger Couillard, c. 1956; 60 x 90 cm; silkscreen. Printed in Canada. CP No. 1707. A6004.

Peter Ewart, c. 1947; 60 x 90 cm; CP silkscreen No. 989. A6353.

Peter Ewart, 1952; 60 x 90 cm; photolithograph. Lithographed in Canada. CP No. 1343. A6354.

Anonymous, c. 1950; 64 x 102 cm; CP silkscreen No. 1188. A6042.

Peter Ewart, c. 1946; 61 x 92 cm; CP silkscreen No. 907. A6524.

Thomas Hall, 1941; 60 x 90 cm; CP silkscreen No. 666. A6693.

James Crockart, c. 1954; 62 x 92 cm; CP silkscreen No. 1472.
UBC-Chung coll. 4034.

Norman Fraser, 1946; 60 x 90 cm; CP silkscreen No. 887. A6388.

Peter Ewart, c. 1950; 60 x 90 cm; CP silkscreen No. 1131. A6544.

Travel *Canadian Pacific*

James Crockart, c. 1946; 60 x 90 cm; CP silkscreen No. 905. A6677.

Roger Couillard, 1955; 60 x 90 cm; lithograph. Lithographed In Canada. A6118.

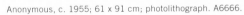

Anonymous, c. 1955; 61 x 91 cm; photolithograph. A6666.

Anonymous, 1964; 60 x 90 cm; CP silkscreen. A6110.

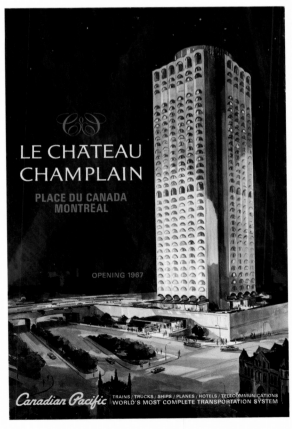

Anonymous, c. 1966; 61 x 91 cm; photolithograph. A6180.

Anonymous, c. 1965; 60 x 91 cm; photolithograph. Printed in Canada. P2818. A6178.

VOYAGEZ
Canadien Pacifique

TRAINS/CAMIONNAGE/BATEAUX/AVIONS/HOTELS/TÉLÉCOMMUNICATIONS—LA COMPAGNIE DE TRANSPORT LA PLUS COMPLÈTE DU MONDE

Peter Ewart, c. 1955; 60 x 90 cm; lithograph. Coll. Marc H. Choko.

Peter Ewart, 1953; 60 x 90 cm; lithograph. Courtesy of Mrs. Linda Ewart.

Anonymous, 1947; 60 x 90 cm; lithograph. Lithographed in Canada. A6699.
The Canadian International Trade Fair banner was silkscreened on top of the lithograph in 1948.

Bern Hill, c. 1950; 60 x 90 cm; CP silkscreen No. 1138. A6277.

Peter Ewart, 1956; 60 x 90 cm; lithograph.
Bulman Bros., B.C. Ltd., Vancouver. Coll. Peter Ewart.

Peter Ewart, 1956; 60 x 90 cm; lithograph.
Bulman Bros., B.C. Ltd., Vancouver. A6673.

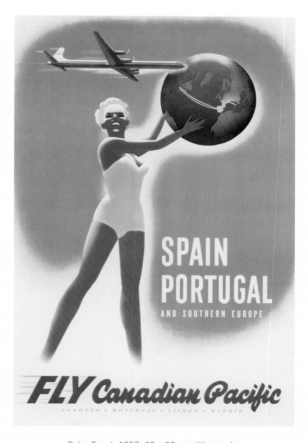

Peter Ewart, 1957; 60 x 90 cm; lithograph.
Bulman Bros., B.C. Ltd., Vancouver. A6525.

Anonymous, c. 1956; 61 x 92 cm; lithograph. Bulman Bros., B.C. Ltd., Vancouver. UBC-Chung coll. 6391.

Anonymous, 1960; 61 x 97 cm; lithograph. Printed in England. Coll. Marc H. Choko.

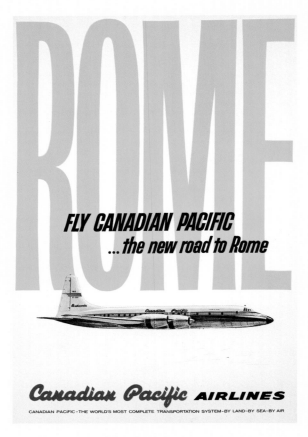

Anonymous, 1960; 60 x 90 cm; lithograph. A6262.

Anonymous, 1960; 61 x 97 cm; lithograph. Printed in England.
Coll. Marc H. Choko.

After Sasek, c. 1965; 59 x 87 cm; lithograph. Printed in Hong Kong
for the Hong Kong Tourist Association. UBC-Chung coll. 4076.

Anonymous, 1970; 61 x 92 cm; lithograph. A6672.

Peter Ewart, 1956; 60 x 90 cm; lithograph. McGill University, RBSC.

William H. Barribal, c. 1930; 60 x 92 cm; lithograph. A6034.

THE ARTISTS: BIOGRAPHICAL NOTES

Biographical information about commercial artists is usually difficult to come by, and this seems to be particularly true of those artists who plied their trade in Canada. While there is a wealth of literature about posters, most often it deals with their design, quality and significance, rather than with the artists and techniques used to produce the posters, and none covered Canadian posters.

In the case of Canadian Pacific, no records exist of the numerous artists commissioned throughout the years, although those whose signatures appear again and again on posters must once have been familiar faces around the poster studio. From the company's registers, it appears that only two artists were employed full-time during the 1930s and 1940s: Gordon Gillespie and Charles Greenwood. The most prolific artist by far of that era was Norman Fraser, but he never appeared on the payroll and nothing is known about him.

Biographical directories, though varied and numerous, tend to include only those artists who were known through the exhibition of their oil or watercolour paintings. For this reason artists such as Alfred Leighton are often listed, while other artists such as Tom Purvis, who was one of the most accomplished and prolific graphic artists of his time, are rarely mentioned.

Through extreme good fortune – and a good collection of Canadian telephone directories – two of the artists, the late Roger Couillard and Peter Ewart, were located in the late 1980s. They were kind enough to make themselves available for interviews and provided documentation that shed new light on the activities of Canadian Pacific in the field of poster art.

Finally, the posters themselves presented a few stumbling blocks – initials and symbols in place of signatures. Unfortunately, these puzzles remain unsolved.

ASHBURNER, A.W. (no information)

BALITIPLIS, W.S. (no information)

BARRIBAL, William H.
Barribal worked as a figure painter, interior studio painter and print illustrator in London, where he held regular exhibitions between 1919 and 1938. His paintings were shown at the Royal Academy of Arts in 1917 and 1919. He designed railway posters for the LNER (London North Eastern Railway). A poster for The Royal Mail Line to New York is reproduced in *Posters and Their Designers* (1924), p. 115.

BURGER, Carl (no information)

BOOK, W. (no information)

COUILLARD, Roger
Couillard was born in Montreal on March 21, 1910. After the tenth grade he attended the École des Beaux-Arts in Montreal for one year. He then decided to leave school to begin a commercial practice, and worked for two years as a church and theatre decorator for Salette et Fils of Montreal. In 1932 Couillard became decorator for the Matou Botté, a popular cabaret.

When Nesbitt-Thompson took over Ogilvy's department stores, Couillard became the decorator for the

W. Book, c. 1930; 55 x 86 cm; lithograph. A6120.

Montreal outlet, further increasing his involvement with commercial art. Visits to New York and Chicago were made to compare styles and window display designs. In 1935 the Institute of Foreign Travel organized a poster competition on the theme of "See Europe Next." Couillard's poster was among those chosen and exhibited in Ogilvy's.

By 1937 he had opened his own studio in Montreal. To attract commissions from both French and English clients, he operated under the name Studio Coutrey. Couillard started to create his own poster designs, and offered them to a variety of companies. Before the end of the year he had reworked his Europe poster for Canadian Pacific. It became "See Europe Next by *Empress of Britain*." John Murray Gibbon, the CPR's general publicity agent, was impressed by Couillard's work and immediately had copies of the poster printed for distribution. The next year Couillard produced "Alaska" for Canadian Pacific. But the company never became as important to him as did its rival, Canadian National Railways, which commissioned a dozen posters from his studio.

During this period Couillard also produced posters for the City of Montreal and the Province of Quebec. In 1943 he joined the Royal Canadian Air Force. He was granted leave periodically to work for the Ardeel Advertising Agency, the firm that had the contract with the Department of War for the Canadian war bonds publicity campaign. He created a half-dozen posters, for which he was paid $100 each (in war bonds).

In 1945 Couillard left the army and returned to his commercial art practice in Montreal. Two years later he moved his studio to Sainte-Adèle, Quebec. Again, most of his commissions were done for a Canadian Pacific competitor – Canadian Steamship Lines – but he was involved in a number of CP advertising campaigns: creating the "White Empress to Europe" poster (1950), among others; executing some large maps for use in railway passenger coaches in the mid-1950s; and contributing to the Canadian Pacific display in the railway pavilion at Toronto's Canadian National Exhibition in 1948. Most of his production work was done by General Advertising, the Hirsch family printing company located in Lachine, Quebec.

In 1952 he won the poster competition that celebrated Newfoundland's entry into Confederation three years earlier. With the expansion of colour photography and the drop in the market for graphic designs, Couillard became involved in the hotel business. In 1957 he was named president of the Hotel Montclair in Sainte-Adèle, Quebec. In 1964 he transferred to the Chantecler Hotel, where he served as vice-president and general manager. Couillard joined the Quebec Ministry of Tourism in 1966, where he became inspector for hotels, retiring from that position in 1975. He died in Sainte-Marguerite on November 18, 1999.

CROCKART, James
Crockart was born in Stirling, Scotland. He attended the Edinburgh College of Art and the Glasgow School of Art. After immigrating to Canada in 1911, Crockart worked for Shagpat Studios in Montreal from 1920 until 1925. After opening his own studio in downtown Montreal, he designed his first poster for Canadian Pacific in 1927 and produced several others during the 1930s and into the early 1950s. In 1939 he was in charge of fifty artists, designers, carpenters and mechanical technicians who were responsible for CPR's exhibit at the New York World's Fair.

DANE, Clement
Dane's studio is credited with the production of the superb *Empress of Britain* poster showing a bow-on view of the ship. It was reproduced in *Modern Publicity* (1932; illustr. no 16) and in Leonard Richmond's *The Technique of the Poster* (1933).

ERNY, E. (no information)

EWART, Peter
Peter Ewart was born on April 7, 1918, in the village of Kisbey, Saskatchewan. His parents were greatly interested in the visual arts, and they encouraged Peter when he showed an avid interest in drawing and colouring. By the time he graduated from West Hill High School in Montreal, he had decided that he wanted to be a professional artist. He took a two-year correspondence course in commercial illustration and attended classes at both Sir George Williams College in Montreal (now Concordia University) and the Art Association of Montreal (now Musée des Beaux Arts). In 1938, with his parents' help, he enrolled in the Commercial Illustration Studio of New York City. The school emphasized the avant-garde work of such designers as A.M. Cassandre, E. McKnight Kauffer, Joseph Binder and Tom Purvis.

The outbreak of the Second World War prevented further study, so Ewart returned to Montreal, put together a portfolio and made the rounds of advertising agencies. Roger Couillard of Studio Coutrey liked his samples and suggested that he show them to the CPR. The result was a commission to do finished artwork for the 1939 poster "Sports d'Hiver." That poster marked the beginning of a twenty-year working relationship in which he designed twenty-four posters and two serigraphic prints.

In 1943 Ewart joined the Royal Canadian Air Force as a wireless operator and served in this capacity for the next three years. When he returned to Montreal after the war, he resumed his work with the expanded Public Relations Department at the CPR. A new interest was now emerging: painting. He showed some of his oil sketches to Gerald Stevens of the Stevens Art Gallery, and soon his paintings were being sold through the gallery.

The Canadian Rockies and the West Coast had appealed to the artist ever since his assignment to RCAF stations in the West. He moved to Vancouver in 1947, established a studio, and divided his time between commercial designing and painting. Ewart continued to design posters for the CPR in Montreal as well as for Canadian Pacific Airlines in Vancouver. He died in Surrey, British Columbia, January 28, 2001.

F. (in a circle or a lozenge). Attributed to Norman Fraser

FINCH, W.C. (no information)

de FOREST
His "Homeward Bound" poster for CPR appears in Leonard Richmond's book *The Technique of the Poster.*

FRASER, Norman
Although Norman Fraser was by far the most prolific artist commissioned by Canadian Pacific, he has remained an elusive figure. We do know that he lived in Montreal from 1930 to 1953 and that he was commissioned to design dozens of posters in that period. He experimented with photomontage and opaque and transparent paint techniques. On a number of posters the artist is identified with an "F" – sometimes in a circle or a lozenge. As the style of these posters is similar to Fraser's, it seems likely that they were also executed by him.

GARDNER, Fred
Gardner was born in Syracuse, New York, on April 16, 1880. He studied at the Pratt Institute Art School in Brooklyn and became a member of the Art Students League in New York. A designer and an architect, he was also recognized as a painter. In the 1920s he was still living and practising in Brooklyn. He was awarded numerous prizes for his work in the 1940s.

GILLESPIE, Gordon Fraser
Born in Montreal on December 5, 1891, Gillespie became an office boy at Canadian Pacific at the age of 14. In 1913 he started his artistic career with the CPR's Exhibits Branch. In 1948 John Murray Gibbon, CPR's general publicity agent, hired him as the art director in charge of all commercial art production. After retiring in January 1957, Gillespie moved to Shelburne, Ontario, where he died on March 26, 1965.

GREENWOOD, Charles James
Greenwood was born in Brantford, Yorkshire, England, on September 22, 1893. After studying at the Brantford School of Art, he moved to Canada, where he settled in Verdun, Quebec. Between November 1924 and March 1940 he worked for Canadian Pacific as a commissioned artist. On March 1, 1940, he was hired as a full-time artist by the Exhibits Branch. Greenwood retired on July 1, 1956, and died on March 1, 1965.

GRIBBLE, Bernard Finegan
Gribble was born in 1873 (some say 1872) in London, England. He was trained as an architect, but also earned a reputation as a painter of oils and watercolours after classes at the South Kensington Art School. He became famous for his marine subjects and exhibited his work at the annual show of the Poole and East Dorset Art Society (of which he eventually became president) and elsewhere. His paintings were present at nearly all exhibitions of the Royal Academy of Arts, from 1905 to 1941. He also worked as an illustrator for *The Illustrated London News* and *The Graphic,* and his work appeared on book covers, postcards and chocolate boxes. He died in Poole in February 1962.

GRIER, Edmund Geoffrey
Born in 1900 in Toronto, Grier was the son of Sir Wyly Grier, a prominent Canadian portrait painter. He was

educated at the Pennsylvania Academy of the Fine Arts. He then worked as a commercial artist, and in 1924 became art director for *Motor Age* magazine in New York. After working as art director for a publishing company in Philadelphia, he returned to Canada, where at the start of the Second World War he settled in Montreal. He was the art director of a leading advertising firm, and in 1943 became a member of the Royal Canadian Academy of Arts. Grier died in Ottawa in 1965.

HALL, Thomas
Hall was born in 1885 at Ackworth, Yorkshire, England. He studied under George Bridgeman at the Art Students League in New York. In 1907 he came to Canada and settled in the Montreal area where, between 1934 and 1954, he had a commercial art studio on Victoria Avenue. He served as vice-president of the Guild of Canadian Commercial Artists. In 1965 he was commissioned to paint a portrait of Winston Churchill for a commemorative folder. Hall's main area of expertise was painting wildlife, a theme that figured in posters produced for Canadian Industries Limited (CIL) and Canadian Pacific. His 1938 grizzly poster for Canadian Pacific won him the Transit Advertisers' award for finest poster in the travel division.

HAMILTON, Edward
Two of his posters for the Royal Mail Line to New York and South America appear in *Posters and Their Designers*.

H.B. (no information)

HICKS, V.
A poster by Hicks appears in *Posters and Their Designers*.

HILL, Bern (no information)

HOLLING, R. (no information)

JACKSON, Alexander Young
Jackson was born on October 3, 1882, in Montreal. At the age of 13 he started work as an office boy for a lithography company. His boss noticed his sketches, and Jackson was moved to the art department under Arthur Nantel. He worked there for six years and then took a job as a designer for a printing house before working at a photo-engraving company and a lithography firm. He attended classes at the Monument National and occasionally visited the Montreal Art Gallery.

At the age of 23, Jackson travelled to London and Paris, then worked in Chicago as a designer while taking evening classes at the Art Institute of Chicago. By September 1907 he was back in Paris, where he studied for six months at the Académie Julian under Jean-Paul Laurens. In 1910 he returned to Canada and worked as a photo-engraver for one year before leaving again for France. His career as an artist was starting and, back in Canada once more, he exhibited with Randolph Hewton at the Art Association of Montreal.

After travelling and painting in Ontario he was introduced to Tom Thomson, and in January 1914 Jackson moved with Thomson into the Studio Building in Toronto. He enlisted in the army in 1915, serving as a private in the First World War and then as a war artist in the Canadian War Memorials program. He became a full member of the Royal Canadian Academy of Arts.

On May 7, 1920, the first exhibition of the Group of Seven opened at the Art Museum of Toronto. The group included Lawren Harris, Arthur Lismer, J.E.H. MacDonald, Frank Carmichael, Frank H. Johnston, Fred Varley and Jackson. They continued to exhibit together as a group until 1931. The Tate Gallery in London bought a painting by Jackson, the only living Canadian artist to be represented in its collection, at the Wembley Exhibition in 1924.

In 1933 Jackson became a founding member of the Canadian Group of Painters. He died in Kleinburg, Ontario, in 1974.

J. P. G. (no information)

KAUFFMAN, G.Y. (no information)

KIHN, Wilfred Langdon
Wilfred Kihn was born on September 5, 1898, in Brooklyn, New York. In 1916 he became a member of the Art Students League in New York. Kihn travelled extensively through the United States and Canada, painting canvases of North American Indians. During the late 1920s and the 1930s, he designed many posters for the Cunard Line, three of which are reproduced in *The Technique of the Poster*. In Canada, Kihn became well known through exhibitions at the Art Gallery of Montreal and the McGill

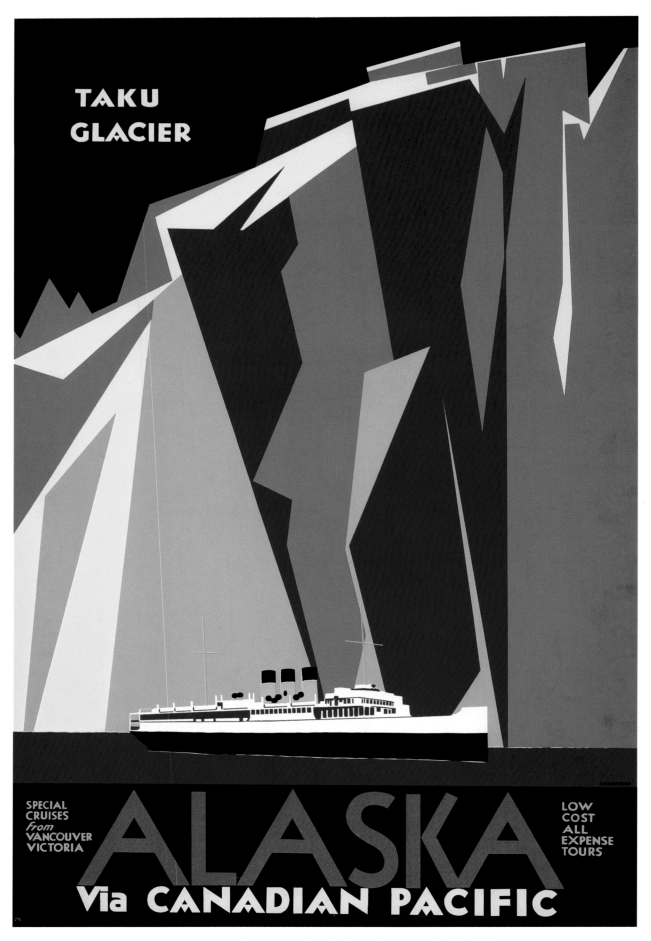

161-1. Charles James Greenwood, c. 1936; 60 x 90 cm; CP silkscreen No. 261. A6584.

University Art Gallery, and various showings in Ottawa, Winnipeg and Vancouver.

LAMY, J. (no information)

LEIGHTON, Alfred Crocker
Alfred Leighton is said to have been born in October 1901 in Hastings, Sussex, England. Although he did not have any formal training, he was successful in obtaining several corporate commissions. One was to design posters and brochure illustrations for the CPR's London office. In the 1920s he worked in western Canada, executing a series of paintings of the Prairies and the Rocky Mountains. His works were exhibited in Calgary and Vancouver in 1928, and in the Royal Academy of Arts Exhibition in London in 1929, 1932, 1933 and 1934.

In 1930 Leighton settled in Calgary and held a major exhibition sponsored by the Hudson's Bay Company. The T. Eaton Company Fine Arts Galleries presented one hundred of his watercolours in 1936. In Calgary he taught at the Institute of Technology and Art and served as president of the Alberta College of Art. Several of his works were featured in the publications *The Studio* and *The Sphere* (both London) and *La Revue Moderne* (Paris). He died in 1965.

LENDON (no information)

LOGAN, Maurice
Maurice Logan was born on February 21, 1886, near Calistoga, California (north of San Francisco). He always wanted to be an artist and started lessons as a child. He trained at the Partington Art School in San Francisco and, after the 1906 earthquake destroyed the school, at the Piedmont Art Gallery. He then joined the San Francisco Institute of Art. He exhibited at the San Francisco Art Association's 1914 annual spring exhibition.

From 1935 to 1943 he taught at the College of Arts and Crafts in Berkeley. After studying at the Art Institute of Chicago, he taught for eight years at the California College of Arts and Crafts at Oakland. A member of the Society of Six, he painted and worked as a commercial artist, illustrating covers for *Sunset* magazine. He died in Orinda, California, on March 22, 1977.

MANN, James Scrymgeour
Mann was born in 1883 in Dundee, Scotland. After serving in the First World War, he studied at the Liverpool School of Art. He came to Liverpool because of his great interest in shipping. He produced postcard artwork for all the main Liverpool maritime companies, including the Cunard Line, White Star and the Bibby Line. In 1942 he was elected president of the Royal Cambrian Academy. He died in Llandudno, Wales, in 1946.

McELROY, George E.
McElroy was born around 1878 in Richmond, Ontario. His father and mother were talented artists, and George began drawing at a very young age. After serving first with the North-West Mounted Police in Regina and then with the Strathcona Horse during the South African War, he became chief of police of Michipicoten Harbour on the north shore of Lake Superior. Eventually he went to the United States, where he became a newspaper illustrator and caricaturist. He became a staff artist with the *St. Paul Globe,* the *St. Louis Post Dispatch* and the *Detroit Free Press.* After returning to Canada he spent six years with the *Montreal Star,* then worked with *La Patrie* and *La Presse.*

McElroy turned to painting subjects related to his own experiences of the Canadian West. He died on August 10, 1945.

McKELL, James C.
American illustrator from Philadelphia, Pennsylvania.

NONG
Most probably an artist of the "School of Shanghai."

PALENSKE, Reinhold H.
Palenske was born in 1884 in Chicago, the son of poor Polish immigrants. Though he attended art school in Chicago, he is thought to be largely self-taught. He became an illustrator for newspapers and a lithographer. He then worked for the Chicago advertising agency Ruthrauf and Ryan, which had an advertising contract with the Canadian Pacific Railway. Assigned to this account, Palenske travelled to western Canada. In 1923 he accompanied John Murray Gibbon, the chief publicist for the CPR, on a trail ride that led to the formation of the Order of the Trail Riders of the Canadian Rockies. He died in Woodstock, Illinois, in 1955.

Norman Fraser, c. 1943; 60 x 90 cm; CP silkscreen No. 750. A6671.

PERRIGARD, Hal Ross

Perrigard was born in 1891 in Montreal. He was interested in art and painted landscape from his early years. He took lessons in drawing from a model at the Royal Canadian Academy of Arts. After a few years in Montreal and Westmount, during which he operated a studio for graphic design, decoration and illustration, he moved to Rockport, Massachussets, in 1923. His artworks were exhibited at the Montreal Spring Show (Salon du Printemps) and he sold a few to the Canadian National Gallery. He created murals for CPR offices and hotels. In 1939 he was commissioned for a mural in the Canadian Pavilion at the New York World's Fair. He had numerous exhibitions and was an active member of various art associations. He died suddenly in 1960.

PURVIS, Tom

Tom Purvis was born in Bristol, England, in 1888. He studied at the Camberwell School of Art, and then went into advertising with Mather and Crowther. During the First World War he became a war artist for the Ministry of Supply. By the late 1920s he had become one of the most prolific and well-known British poster designers, commissioned by London and North Eastern Railway, Shell-Mex, British Petroleum, Austin Reed and Imperial Airways. He served on the committee for the British Art in Industry Exhibition at the Royal Academy in 1935 and in 1946 was made a Royal Designer for Industry. Purvis was appointed vice-president of the Royal Society of Art and became the official poster artist for the British government during the Second World War.

RICHMOND, Leonard

Richmond was born in Somerset, England, in 1878. He studied at the Taunton School of Art and Chelsea Polytechnic, and exhibited at the principal London galleries and abroad. During the First World War, the Canadian government commissioned him to sketch at the front in France. He wrote several books on painting technique and is the author of *The Technique of the Poster*. His paintings were presented nearly every year, from 1920 to 1955, at the Royal Academy of Arts Exhibition.

He lived in London, England, and died in 1965.

RIGAL, Morley (no information)

RITCHIE, Alick P.F.

This prolific English poster artist was famous in the late nineteenth century. Four of his posters (restaurant, store, cabaret, theatre) appear in *L'affiche anglaise: les années 90;* one poster (cabaret) appears in *L'Estampe et l'Affiche,* 15 janvier 1899, 3e année no 1, p. 18.

RODMELL, Harry Hudson

Harry Rodmell was born in England in 1896. He studied at the Hull College of Art and became a watercolourist and oil painter of landscapes and seascapes. Two of his paintings were presented in 1949 at the Royal Academy of Arts Exhibition.

ROSENVINGE, Odin

Of Danish descent, Rosenvinge was born in Newcastle-upon-Tyne, England, in 1880. After a short time as a trainee reporter, he joined a Leeds commercial art and printing firm. In 1912 he moved to Liverpool and joined Turner and Dunett, which had a number of shipping companies as clients. Rosenvinge produced many posters at this time. He served in the Middle East during the First World War and later on became a freelance designer and illustrator. He died in 1957.

SASEK (no information)

SCHLISINGER (no information)

SCHRODER, Robert (no information)

SHOESMITH, Kenneth Denton

Shoesmith was born in Halifax, Yorkshire, England, on April 6, 1890. He took up painting during his travels as a seaman and officer in the British merchant marine. After the First World War, he became a full-time watercolourist and oil painter of marine subjects. He also began to design posters. His works were exhibited in the Royal Academy of Arts Exhibition in 1922 and 1934. He was a member of the British Society of Poster Designers and in 1925 was elected to the Royal Institute of Painters in Water-Colours. He took part in the Paris Salon and had solo exhibitions in Liverpool and Belfast. His posters for the Southern Railway, showing night scenes, were widely distributed and appeared in books such as Richmond's *The Technique of the Poster.* Shoesmith died in London on September 5, 1939.

STAYNES, Percy Angelo

Staynes was born in England in 1875. He studied at the Manchester School of Art, the Royal College of Art and the Académie Julian in Paris. He established himself in London as a watercolourist and oil painter, as well as an illustrator and designer. He was a member of the Royal Institute of Painters in Water-Colours and of the Royal Institute of Oil Painters. During the Second World War, Staynes designed posters for the British campaign against the German U-boats. He died in London on April 14, 1953.

T.F. (no information)

VALENTINE, J.C. (no information)

VICKERY, John (no information)

WARD, Dudley (no information)

WHITE, A.E. (no information)

WHITMORE, Olive (no information)

WILKINSON, Norman

Norman Wilkinson was born in 1878 in Cambridge, England. He studied art at the Portsmouth and Southsea schools of art. After becoming famous as a marine painter and an engraver, he designed posters for the London and North Western Railway (LNWR) and the London, Midland and Scottish Railway (LMS), and worked for the *Illustrated London News* and the *Illustrated Mail*. His paintings were presented nearly every year from 1907 to 1970 at the Royal Academy of Arts Exhibition. He died in 1971.

DATING THE POSTERS

Dating the posters presented a variety of problems. A very small number had the dates recorded on them by the artist or printer, but for the vast majority the dates had to be determined through examination of the subject matter and the styles and techniques used.

In many cases, the posters were created to announce the inauguration of a specific new service or facility – a ship launching, a hotel opening or the introduction of a new railway or airline service. Records within the Canadian Pacific Railway Archives collection allowed these posters to be dated precisely, with minimal difficulty. In the absence of these milestones, company logos, paint schemes and slogans gave some indication of the era in which to place a particular work. Throughout the 1920s the words "lithographed in Canada" or "printed in Canada" appeared on a series of posters. Details in the illustrations, such as the number of a locomotive or the fares for a particular service, helped pinpoint specific years.

Art magazines and CPR staff publications yielded occasional references to posters, particularly if the works had received recognition in the numerous exhibitions and competitions of the 1930s and 1940s. Books on Canadian posters, although rare, seldom fail to include some mention of Canadian Pacific's prodigious output.

Regrettably, the CPR's Exhibits Branch records of payments made to artists no longer exist. Several of the posters designed by Peter Ewart were dated using the detailed records in the artist's possession.

Finally, the numbers assigned to the posters by the Exhibits Branch, which are recorded on many of them, provided a rough chronology. Some care had to be taken when using these indicators, as reprints were sometimes given the next available number rather than the number of the first print run (with "rerun" written beside it). We even found a few different posters bearing the same number.

CANADIAN PACIFIC
EMPRESS OF AUSTRALIA
EUROPE · CANADA · U.S.A.

APPLY—

PICKFORDS LTD.,
95 QUEEN'S ROAD, BRIGHTON.

Alfred Crocker Leighton, c. 1925; 62 x 100 cm; lithograph. Courtesy of Wally Chung.

BIBLIOGRAPHY

BOOKS

Amstutz, Walter, ed. *Who's Who in Graphic Art.* Zurich: Amstutz and Herdeg Graphic Press, 1962.

Bain, Donald. *Canadian Pacific Air Lines: Its History and Aircraft.* Calgary: Kishorn, 1987.

Choko, Marc H. *L'affiche au Québec. Des origines à nos jours.* Montréal: Éditions de l'Homme, 2001.

Dimson, Theo, ed. *Great Canadian Posters.* Toronto: Oxford University Press, 1979.

Fielding, Mantle. *Dictionary of American Painters, Sculptors and Engravers.* New York: Apollo, 1986.

Folk, Peter Hastings, ed. *Who Was Who in American Art.* Madison, CT: Sound View, 1985.

Gibbon, John Murray. *Steel of Empire: The Romantic History of the Canadian Pacific, the Northwest Passage of Today.* Toronto: McClelland & Stewart, 1935.

Green, Oliver. *Art for the London Underground.* New York: Rizzoli, 1990.

Ham, George Henry. *Reminiscences of a Raconteur.* Toronto: Musson, 1921.

Harlice, Patricia Pate. *Index to Canadian Biography.* Metuchen, NJ.: Scarecrow Press, 1973.

Harper, J. Russell. *Early Painters and Engravers in Canada.* Toronto: University of Toronto Press, 1970.

Hart, E.J. *The Selling of Canada: The CPR and the Beginnings of Canadian Tourism.* Banff, AB: Altitude, 1983.

Hedges, James B. *Building the Canadian West: The Land and Colonization Policies of the Canadian Pacific Railway.* New York: Macmillan, 1935.

Hughes, Edan Milton. *Artists in California. 1786–1940.* San Francisco: Hughes Publishing, 1986.

MacDonald, Colin S. *Dictionary of Canadian Artists.* Ottawa: Canadian Paperbacks, 1977.

Musée de la Publicité. *L'Affiche anglaise: les années '90.* Paris, 1972 (catalogue).

Richmond, Leonard. *The Technique of the Poster.* London: Pitman, 1933.

Royal Academy Exhibitors. 1905–1970. A Dictionary of Artists and Their Work in the Summer Exhibitions of Royal Academy of Arts. East Ardsley (England): EP Publishing, 1982.

Shackleton, J.T. *The Golden Age of the Railway Poster.* London: New English Library, 1976.

Stacey, Robert. *The Canadian Poster Book.* Toronto: Methuen, 1982.

Waters, Grant M. *Dictionary of British Artists Working 1900–1950.* Sussex: Eastbourne Fine Art, 1975.

Weill, Alain. *The Poster.* Boston: Hall, 1985.

PERIODICALS

Art and Industry. Vol. 22 (131), 1937; vol. 25 (146), 1938.

Art and Publicity. 1925.

Canadian Pacific Staff Bulletin. Aug. 1, 1935; Jan. 5, 1941; Feb. 5, 1941; Jan. 5, 1943; May 5, 1943; Oct. 5, 1943.

Commercial Art. Vol. 2 (8), 1927.

Commercial Art and Industry. Vol. 12 (72), 1932.

Modern Publicity. 1930–1960.

Posters and Publicity. 1926–1929.

Posters and Their Designers. 1924.

BROCHURES

Jones, David. *Canadian Pacific Poster Art 1881–1955: An Exhibition of Posters by Canadian Pacific Corporate Archives.* Montreal: Canadian Pacific, 1985.

Several editions of *The Canadian Who's Who* and *Who's Who in Canada* were consulted for biographical details on the artists. Various exhibition and auction catalogues yielded occasional references to specific works. *Lovell's Montreal Street Directory*, published annually, located some of the commercial art studios in that city.

Anonymous, c. 1925; 60 x 93 cm; lithograph. Printed in Canada. A6025.

INDEX